Important Instruction

Use the URL or QR code provided below to unlock all the online learning resources included with this Grade 7 to 8 summer bridge activities workbook.

URL	QR Code
Visit the URL below and place the book access code **http://www.lumoslearning.com/a/tedbooks** **Access Code: G7-8MLSLH-19562**	

Your online access will include;

- Skills practice resources for Grade 8 Math and ELA
- Grade-appropriate passages to improve reading skills
- Grade 7 vocabulary quizzes
- Free entry to Lumos Short Story Competition
- Educational videos, worksheets, mobile apps, standards information and more

Lumos Learning
Developed by Expert Teachers

Summer Learning HeadStart, Grade 7 to 8: Fun Activities Plus Math, Reading, and Language Workbooks

Contributing Author   - Stacy Zeiger
Contributing Author   - Aaron Spencer
Contributing Author   - Julie C. Lyons
Contributing Editor   - George Smith
Contributing Editor   - Marisa Adams
Executive Producer   - Mukunda Krishnaswamy
Database Administrator - R. Raghavendra Rao

ISBN 10: 1940484731

ISBN 13: 978-1-940484-73-0

Printed in the United States of America

For permissions and additional information contact us

Lumos Information Services, LLC
PO Box 1575, Piscataway, NJ 08855-1575
http://www.LumosLearning.com

Email: support@lumoslearning.com
Tel: (732) 384-0146
Fax: (866) 283-6471

Lumos Learning
Developed by Expert Teachers

Table of Contents

Introduction

What is Summer Academic Learning Loss?

Studies show that if students take a standardized test at the end of the school year, and then repeat that test when they return in the fall, they will lose approximately four to six weeks of learning. In other words, they could potentially miss more questions in the fall than they would in the spring. This loss is commonly referred to as the summer slide.

When these standardized testing scores drop an average of one month it causes teachers to spend at least the first four to five weeks, on average, re-teaching critical material. In terms of math, students typically lose an average of two and a half months of skills and when reading and math losses are combined, it averages three months; it may even be lower for students in lower income homes.

And on average, the three areas students will typically lose ground in are spelling, vocabulary, and mathematics.

How can You Help Combat Summer Learning Loss?

Like anything, academics are something that require practice and if they are not used regularly, you run the risk of losing them. Because of this, it is imperative your children work to keep their minds sharp over the summer. There are many ways to keep your children engaged over the summer and we're going to explore some of the most beneficial.

Start with School:

Your best source of information is your child's school. Have a conversation with your child's teacher. Tell them you are interested in working on some academics over the summer and ask what suggestions they might have. Be sure to ask about any areas your child may be struggling in and for a list of books to read over the summer. Also, talk to your child's counselor. They may have recommendations of local summer activities that will relate back to the schools and what your child needs to know. Finally, ask the front office staff for any information on currently existing after school programs (the counselor may also be able to provide this). Although after school programs may end shortly, the organizations running them will often have information on summer camps. Many of these are often free or at a very low cost to you and your family.

Stay Local:

Scour your local area for free or low cost activities and events. Most museums will have dollar days of some kind where you can get money off admission for going a certain day of the week, or certain time. Zoos will often do the same thing. Take lunch to the park and eat outside, talking about the leaves, flowers, or anything else you can find there. Your child can pick one favorite thing and research it. Attend concerts or shows put on by local artists, musicians, or other vendors.
There are many, many other options available, you just have to explore and find them. The key here is to engage your children. Have them look online with you or search the local newspapers/magazines. Allow them to plan the itinerary, or work with you on it, and when they get back, have them write a journal about the activity. Or, even better, have them write a letter or email to a family member about what they did.

Practice Daily:

Whether the choice is a family activity, experiencing the local environment, or staying academically focused the key is to keep your child engaged every day. That daily practice helps keep students' minds sharp and focused, ensuring they will be able to not only retain the knowledge they have learned, but in many cases begin to move ahead for the next year.

Summer Strategies for Students

Summer is here which brings a time of excitement, relaxation, and fun. School is the last thing on your mind, but that doesn't mean learning has to be on vacation too. In fact, learning is as just as important, and be just as fun (if not more), during the summer months than during the school year.

Did you know that during the summer:

- Students often lose an average of 2 and ½ months of math skills
- Students often lose 2 months of reading skills
- Teachers spend at least the first 4 to 5 weeks of the next school year reteaching important skills and concepts

Your brain is like a muscle, and like any muscle, it must be worked out regularly, and like this, your language arts and math skills are something that requires practice; if you do not use them regularly, you run the risk of losing them. So, it is very important you keep working through the summer. But, it doesn't always have to be 'school' type work. There are many ways to stay engaged, and we're going to spend a little time looking through them.

Read and Write as Often as Possible

Reading is one of the most important things you can do to keep your brain sharp and engaged. Here are some tips to remember about summer reading:

- Often, summer is the perfect time to find and read new books or books you have always been curious about. However, without your teacher, you may struggle with finding a book that is appropriate for your reading level. In this case, you just have to remember the five finger rule: open a book to a random page and begin reading aloud, holding up one finger for each word you cannot say or do not know. If you have more than five fingers visible, the book is probably too hard.

- Reading goes beyond books; there are so many other ways to read. Magazines are a great way to keep kids connected to learning, and they encourage so many different activities. National Geographic Kids, Ranger Rick, and American Girl are just a few examples. As silly as it may sound, you can also read the backs of cereal boxes and billboards to work on reading confidence and fluency, and learn many new things along the way! And thinking completely outside the box, you can also read when singing karaoke. Reading the words as they flash across the screen is a great way to build fluency. You can also turn the closed captioning on when a TV show is on to encourage literacy and reading fluency.

But writing is equally as important, and there are many things you can do to write over the summer:

- First, consider keeping a journal of you summer activities. You can detail the things you do, places you go, even people you meet. Be sure to include as much description as possible – sights, sounds, colors should all be included so you can easily remember and visualize the images. But the wonderful thing about a journal is that spelling and sentence structure are not as important. It's just the practice of actually writing that is where your focus should be. The other nice thing about a journal is that this informal writing is just for you; with journal writing you don't have to worry about anything, you just want to write.

- But if you want a little more depth to your journaling, and you want to share it with others, there is a fantastic opportunity for you with blogging. With parental approval, you can create a blog online where you can share your summer experiences with friends, family, or any others. The wonderful thing about blogs is that you can play with the privacy settings and choose who you want to see your blogs. You can make it private, where only the individuals who you send the link to can see it, or you can choose for it to be public where anyone can read it. Of course, if you are keeping a blog, you will have to make it a little more formal and pay attention to spelling, grammar, and sentences simply because you want to make sure your blog is pleasing to those who are reading it. Some popular places to post blogs are Blogger, Wordpress, Squarespace, and Quillpad.

Practice Math in Real Life

One way you can keep your brain sharp is by looking at that world around you and finding ways to include math. In this case, we're thinking of fun, practical ways to practice in your daily life.

- First, have some fun this summer with being in charge of some family projects. Suggest a fun project to complete with a parent or grandparent; decide on an area to plant some new bushes or maybe a small home project you can work on together. You can help design the project and maybe even research the best plants to plant or the best way to build the project. Then write the shopping list, making sure you determine the correct amount of supplies you will need. Without even realizing it, you will have used some basic math calculations and geometry to complete the project.

- You can also find math in shopping for groceries or while doing some back to school shopping. For each item that goes into the cart, estimate how much it will be and keep a running estimation of the total cost. Make it a competition before you go by estimating what your total bill will be and see who comes the closest. Or, you can even try and compete to see who can determine the correct total amount of tax that will be needed. And a final mental game to play while shopping is to determine the change you should receive when paying with cash. Not only is this a good skills to practice, it, more importantly, helps you make sure you're getting the correct change.

- You can even use everyday math if you are doing any traveling this summer and there are many fun ways to do this. Traveling requires money, and someone has to be in charge of the budget. You can volunteer to be the family accountant. Make a budget for the trip and keep all the receipts. Tally up the cost of the trip and even try to break it up by category – Food, fun, hotels, gas are just a few of the categories you can include. For those of you that might be looking for even more of a challenge, you can calculate what percentage of your budget has been spent on each category as well.

- And traveling by car gives many opportunities as well. Use the car odometer to calculate how far you have traveled. For an added challenge, you can see if you can calculate how much gas you used as well as how many gallons of gas per mile have been used.

Practice Daily:

Whether the choice is a family activity, experiencing the local environment, or staying academically focused the key is to keep your mind engaged every day. That daily practice helps keeps your brain sharp and focused, and helps ensure you will be able to not only retain the knowledge you learned last year but get a jump start on next year's success too!

How to Use this Book Effectively

A combination of Math and English language arts activities help students explore the various standards, review content, and keep academic skills sharp. And for students who enjoy a challenge and want to get a jump on the next school year, the next grade level online workbook is accessible to your child.

Remember, you should:

- Familiarize yourself with the struggles of the summer slide.
- Encourage daily learning
- Review student work in the Summer Learning HeadStart Grade 7 to 8 workbook.
- Help your child explore next year's content in the Lumos StepUp Online Workbooks by following the instructions in "Online Program Benifits" section of this chapter.
- Help your student download the Lumos StepUp app using the instructions provided in "How to download the Lumos StepUp App" section of this chapter.
- Review your student's reading assignment online.
- Review your student's vocabulary assignment online.
- Review your student's weekly summer diary.
- You can also conveniently access student progress report on your mobile devices by downloading the Lumos StepUp app. Please follow directions provided in "How can I Download the App?" section in Lumos StepUp® Mobile App FAQ For Parents and Teachers.
- Keep summer learning as fun and engaging as possible!

Lumos Short Story Competition 2019

**Write a Short Story
Based On Your Summer Experiences**

Get A Chance To Win $100 Cash Prize

1 Year Free Subscription To Lumos StepUp

Trophy With Certificate

How can my child participate in this competition?

Step 1

Visit **www.lumoslearning.com/a/tedbooks** and enter your access code to create Lumos parent account and student account.

Access Code : G7-8MLSLH-19562

Or Scan the QR code to register

Step 2

After registration, your child can upload their summer story by logging into the student portal and clicking on **Lumos Short Story Competition 2019.**
Last date for submission is August 31, 2019

How is this competition judged?

Lumos teachers will review students submissions in Sep 2019. Quality of submission would be judged based on creativity, coherence and writing skills.
We recommend short stories that are less than 500 words.

Unit Rates (7.R.P.A.1)

1. If y is proportional to x, and y = 4 when x = 6, what is the constant of proportionality between them (the ratio of x to y)?

    Ⓐ $\dfrac{4}{6}$

    Ⓑ $\dfrac{2}{3}$

    ● $\dfrac{3}{2}$

    Ⓓ 3

2. John eats a bowl of cereal for 3 of his 4 meals each day. He finishes two gallons of milk in eight days. How much milk does John use for one bowl of cereal? (Assume he only uses the milk for his cereal.)

    ● One-twelfth of a gallon of milk
    Ⓑ One cup of milk
    Ⓒ Two cups of milk
    Ⓓ One-sixth of a gallon of milk

3. A recipe to make a cake calls for three fourths of a cup of milk. Mary used this cake as the first layer of a wedding cake. The second layer was half the size of the first layer, and the third layer was half the size of the second layer. How much milk would be used for the entire wedding cake?

    Ⓐ one and two-thirds cups of milk
    Ⓑ one and one-third cups of milk
    ● one and five-sixteenths cups of milk
    Ⓓ one cup of milk

Day 1

From *Scouting for Boys*

"Hi! Stop Thief!" shouted old Blenkinsopp as he rushed out of his little store near the Kaffir village. "He's stolen my sugar. Stop him."

Stop whom? There was nobody in sight running away, "Who stole it?" asked the policeman.

"I don't know, but a whole bag of sugar is missing. It was there only a few minutes ago." A native police tracker was called in and it looked a pretty impossible job for him to single out the tracks of the thief from among dozens of other footprints about the store. However, he presently started off hopeful, at a jog-trot, away out into the bush. In some places he went over hard stony ground, but he never checked his pace, although no footmarks could be seen. People wondered how he could possibly find the trail. Still he trotted on. Old Blenkinsopp was feeling the heat and the pace.

At length the tracker suddenly stopped and cast around having evidently lost the trail. Then a grin came on his face as he pointed with his thumb over his shoulder up the tree near which he was standing. There, concealed among the branches, they saw a native with the missing bag of sugar.

How had the tracker spotted him? His sharp eyes had described some grains of sugar sparkling in the dust. The bag leaked, leaving a slight trail of these grains. He followed that trail and when it came to an end in the bush the tracker noticed a string of ants going up a tree. They were after the sugar, and so was he, and between them they brought about the capture of the thief.

Old Blenkinsopp was so pleased that he promptly opened the bag and spilled a lot of the sugar on the ground as a reward to the ants.

I expect that he also patted the tracker on the back for his cleverness in using his eyes to see the grains of sugar and the ants, and in using his wits to see why the ants were climbing the tree.

4. Why could the policeman not find the footprints from among the others in the shop?

- Ⓐ because they were clearly marked
- ● there were dozens of footprints
- Ⓒ there were no footprints to be found
- Ⓓ the footprints had been cleaned

Tryouts

For years, Sam had dreamed of being the best tennis player in the world. He went to tennis practice every single morning, and every single night. He spent every summer at tennis camp, and he gave up long weekends at the beach to work on his game. Now, it seemed his hard work was finally paying off: He was invited to try out for the state tennis team!

Still, there was something that was bothering Sam. The tryouts for the tennis team were on the same day as his mom's birthday, and he knew his family was planning a huge surprise party for her. He didn't want to hurt his mom's feelings by missing the party, but he also didn't want to miss his one shot at being a champion tennis player. He was in a quandary; he didn't know what to do.

For days, Sam went to bed worrying about the decision. If he went to the tryout, he worried he would seem selfish. If he stayed home, he would miss his one big shot at making the state team. In fact, despite the honor of being invited to try out, he hadn't even told his family about the opportunity. He was so stressed about making the decision of whether to go or not that he couldn't even think about sharing the news.

Weeks went by, and Sam was making no progress. Every day his coach asked him if he was ready for the tryout, and Sam couldn't even respond. Finally, Sam couldn't bear the stress any longer. He decided to talk to his grandfather about his predicament.

"You know, your mom wants you to be happy," he told Sam. "It would be a great birthday present for her to know you are making your dream come true."

Sam had never thought of it that way before, and after talking to his grandfather, he knew what he had to do. He immediately went home and sat down with his parents to let them know about the opportunity to try out for the state team. When Sam apologetically told his parents what day the tryouts were, they were so busy shrieking with excitement that he thought maybe they hadn't heard.

"But Mom, that means I'm going to miss your birthday," Sam said. "I am happy you are being so nice about it, but I still feel really bad."

"Are you kidding?" his mom asked? "This is the best present I could ask for!"

5. In this passage, who helps Sam make his choice?

Ⓐ His dog
Ⓑ His neighbor
Ⓒ His grandfather
Ⓓ His mom

Understanding and Representing Proportions(7.RP.A.2.A)

Day 2

1. The following table shows two variables in a proportional relationship:

a	b
2	6
3	9
4	12

   Which of the following is an algebraic statement showing the relationship between a and b.

   Ⓐ a = 3b
   Ⓑ b = 3a
   Ⓒ b = 1/3 (a)
   Ⓓ a = 1/2 (b)

2. If the ratio of the length of a rectangle to its width is 3 to 2, what is the length of a rectangle whose width is 4 inches?

   Ⓐ 4 in.
   Ⓑ 5 in.
   Ⓒ 6 in.
   Ⓓ 7 in.

3. The following table shows two variables in a proportional relationship:

e	f
5 ×5	25
6	30
7	35

   Using the relationship between e and f as shown in this table, find the value of f when e = 11..

   Ⓐ 40
   Ⓑ 45
   Ⓒ 50
   Ⓓ 55

Day 2

"The Lament"
by Srvani

It is twilight. A thick wet snow is slowly twirling around the newly lighted street lamps and lying in soft thin layers on roofs, on horses' backs, on people's shoulders and hats. The cabdriver, Iona Potapov, is quite white and looks like a phantom: he is bent double as far as a human body can bend double; he is seated on his box; he never makes a move. If a whole snowdrift fell on him, it seems as if he would not find it necessary to shake it off. His little horse is also quite white, and remains motionless; its immobility, its angularity and its straight wooden-looking legs, even close by, give it the appearance of a gingerbread horse worth a kopek. It is, no doubt, plunged in deep thought. If you were snatched from the plough, from your usual gray surroundings, and were thrown into this slough full of monstrous lights, unceasing noise and hurrying people, you too would find it difficult not to think.

Iona and his little horse have not moved from their place for a long while. They left their yard before dinner and, up to now, not a fare. The evening mist is descending over the town, the white lights of the lamps are replacing brighter rays, and the hubbub of the street is getting louder.

'Cabby for Viborg Way!' suddenly hears Iona. 'Cabby!'
Iona jumps and, through his snow-covered eyelashes, sees an officer in a greatcoat, with his hood over his head.

'Viborg way!' the officer repeats. 'Are you asleep, eh? Viborg way!'
With a nod of assent Iona picks up the reins, in consequence of which layers of snow slip off the horse's back and neck. The officer seats himself in the sleigh, the cabdriver smacks his lips to encourage his horse, stretches out his neck like a swan, sits up and, more from habit than necessity, brandishes his whip. The little horse also stretches its neck, bends its wooden-looking legs, and makes a move undecidedly.

'What are you doing, werewolf!' is the exclamation Iona hears from the dark mass moving to and fro, as soon as they have started.
'Where the devil are you going? To the r-r-right!'

'You do not know how to drive. Keep to the right!' calls the officer angrily. A coachman from a private carriage swears at him; a passerby, who has run across the road and rubbed his shoulder against the horse's nose, looks at him furiously as he sweeps the snow from his sleeve. Iona shifts about on his seat as if he was on needles, moves his elbows as if he were trying to keep his equilibrium, and gasps about like someone suffocating, who does not understand why and wherefore he is there.

'What scoundrels they all are!' jokes the officer; 'one would think they had all entered into an agreement to jostle you or fall under your horse.'

Iona looks around at the officer and moves his lips. He evidently wants to say something but the only sound that issues is a snuffle.

'What?' asks the officer.

Iona twists his mouth into a smile and, with an effort, says hoarsely: 'My son, Barin, died this week.'

Hm! What did he die of?'

Iona turns with his whole body towards his fare and says: 'And who knows! They say high fever. He was three days in the hospital and then died… God's will be done.'

"Turn round! The devil!' sounds from the darkness. 'Have you popped off, old doggie, eh? Use your eyes!'

'Go on, go on,' says the officer, 'otherwise we shall not get there by tomorrow. Hurry up a bit!'

"If you were snatched from the plough, from your usual gray surroundings, and were thrown into this slough full of monstrous lights, unceasing noise and hurrying people, you too would find it difficult not to think."

4. What can be inferred from the first two paragraphs of the passage?

Ⓐ that the cab driver was very sad
Ⓑ that the cabby was from a village or a very small town
Ⓒ that the cab driver did not want to think
Ⓓ that the cab driver was not thinking

"Bruno the Bear"
Excerpt from *The Bond of Love*

I WILL begin with Bruno; my wife's pet sloth bear. I got him for her by an accident. Two years ago we were passing through the cornfields near a small town in Iowa. People were driving away the wild pigs from the fields by shooting at them. Some were shot and some escaped. We thought that everything was over when suddenly a black sloth bear came out panting in the hot sun.

Now I will not shoot a sloth bear wantonly but unfortunately for the poor beast, one of my companions did not feel the same way about it, and promptly shot the bear on the spot.

As we watched the fallen animal we were surprised to see that the black fur on its back moved and left the prostrate body. Then we saw it was a baby bear that had been riding on its mother's back when the sudden shot had killed her. The little creature ran around its prostrate parent making a pitiful noise.

I ran up to it to attempt a capture. It scooted into the sugarcane field. Following it with my companions, I was at last able to grab it by the scruff of its neck while it snapped and tried to scratch me with its long, hooked claws.

We put it in one of the large jute-bags we had brought and when I got back home I duly presented it to my wife. She was delighted! She at once put a blue colored ribbon around its neck, and after discovering the cub was a 'boy' she christened it Bruno.

Bruno soon took to drinking milk from a bottle. It was but a step further and within a very few days he started eating and drinking everything else. And everything is the right word, for he ate porridge made from any ingredients, vegetables, fruit, nuts, meat (especially pork), curry and rice regardless of condiments and chilies, bread, eggs, chocolates, sweets, pudding, ice-cream, etc., etc., etc. As for drink: milk, tea, coffee, lime juice, aerated water, buttermilk, beer, alcoholic liquor and, in fact, anything liquid. It all went down with relish.

The bear became very attached to our two dogs and to all the children living in and around our farm. He was left quite free in his younger days and spent his time in playing, running into the kitchen and going to sleep in our beds.

One day an accident befell him. I put down poison (barium carbonate) to kill the rats and mice that had got into my library. Bruno entered the library as he often did, and ate some of the poison. Paralysis set in to the extent that he could not stand on his feet. But he dragged himself on his stumps to my wife, who called me. I guessed what had happened.

Off I rushed him in the car to the vet's residence. A case of poisoning! Tame Bear—barium carbonate—what to do? Out came his medical books, and a feverish reference to index began: "What poison did you say, sir?" he asked
"Barium carbonate" I said.
"Ah yes—B—Ba—Barium Salts—Ah! Barium carbonate! Symptoms— paralysis—treatment—injections of . .. Just a minute, sir. I'll bring my syringe and the medicine." Said the doc. I dashed back to the car. Bruno was still floundering about on his stumps, but clearly he was weakening rapidly; there was some vomiting, he was breathing heavily, with heaving flanks and gaping mouth. I was really scared and did not know what to do. I was feeling very guilty and was running in and out of the vet's house doing everything the doc asked me.

"Hold him, everybody!" In goes the hypodermic—Bruno squeals — 10 c.c. of the antidote enters his system without a drop being wasted. Ten minutes later: condition unchanged! Another 10 c.c. Injected! Ten minutes later: breathing less torturous— Bruno can move his arms and legs a little although he cannot stand yet. Thirty minutes later: Bruno gets up and has a great feed! He looks at us disdainfully, as much as to say, 'What's barium carbonate to a big black bear like me?' Bruno was still eating. I was really happy to see him recover.

The months rolled on and Bruno had grown many times the size he was when he came. He had equaled the big dogs in height and had even outgrown them. But was just as sweet, just as mischievous, just as playful. And he was very fond of us all. Above all, he loved my wife, and she loved him too! And he could do a few tricks, too. At the command, 'Bruno, wrestle', or 'Bruno, box,' he vigorously tackled anyone who came forward for a rough and tumble. Give him a stick and say 'Bruno, hold gun', and he pointed the stick at you. Ask him, 'Bruno, where's baby?' and he immediately produced and cradled affectionately a stump of wood which he had carefully concealed in his straw bed. But because of the neighborhoods' and our renters' children, poor Bruno, had to be kept chained most of the time.

Then my son and I advised my wife, and friends advised her too, to give Bruno to the zoo. He was getting too big to keep at home. After some weeks of such advice she at last consented. Hastily, and before she could change her mind, a letter was written to the curator of the zoo. Did he want a tame bear for his collection? He replied, "Yes". The zoo sent a cage in a truck, a distance of hundred – eighty – seven miles, and Bruno was packed off.
We all missed him greatly; but in a sense we were relieved. My wife was inconsolable. She wept and fretted. For the first few days she would not eat a thing. Then she wrote a number of letters to the curator. How was Bruno? Back came the replies,
"Well, but fretting; he refuses food too."

After that, friends visiting the zoo were begged to make a point of seeing how Bruno was getting along. They reported that he was well but looked very thin and sad. All the keepers at the zoo said he was fretting. For three months I managed to restrain my wife from visiting the zoo. Then she said one day, "I must see Bruno. Either you take me by car; or I will go myself by bus or train myself." So I took her by car. Friends had conjectured that the bear would not recognize her. I had thought so too. But while she was yet some yards from his cage Bruno saw her and recognized her. He howled with happiness. She ran up to him, petted him through the bars, and he stood on his head in delight.

For the next three hours she would not leave that cage. She gave him tea, lemonade, cakes, ice cream and what not. Then 'closing time' came and we had to leave. My wife cried bitterly; Bruno cried bitterly; even the hardened curator and the keepers felt depressed. As for me, I had reconciled myself to what I knew was going to happen next.

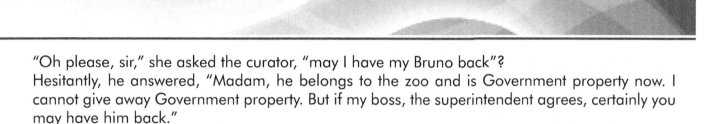

"Oh please, sir," she asked the curator, "may I have my Bruno back"?

Hesitantly, he answered, "Madam, he belongs to the zoo and is Government property now. I cannot give away Government property. But if my boss, the superintendent agrees, certainly you may have him back."

There followed the return journey home and a visit to the superintendent's office. A tearful pleading: "Bruno and I are both fretting for each other. Will you please give him back to me?" He was a kind-hearted man and consented. Not only that, but he wrote to the curator telling him to lend us a cage for transporting the bear back home.

Back we went to the zoo again, armed with the superintendent's letter. Bruno was driven into a small cage and hoisted on top of the car; the cage was tied securely, and a slow and careful return journey back home was accomplished.

Once home, a squad of workers were engaged for special work around our yard. An island was made for Bruno. It was twenty feet long and fifteen feet wide, and was surrounded by a dry moat, six feet wide and seven feet deep. A wooden box that once housed fowls was brought and put on the island for Bruno to sleep in at night. Straw was placed inside to keep him warm, and his 'baby', the gnarled stump, along with his 'gun', the piece of bamboo, both of which had been sentimentally preserved since he had been sent away to the zoo, were put back for him to play with. In a few days the workers hoisted the cage on to the island and Bruno was released. He was delighted; standing on his hind legs, he pointed his 'gun' and cradled his 'baby'. My wife spent hours sitting on a chair there while he sat on her lap. He was fifteen months old and pretty heavy too!

The way my wife reaches the island and leaves it is interesting. I have tied a rope to the overhanging branch of a maple tree with a loop at its end. Putting one foot in the loop, she kicks off with the other, to bridge the six-foot gap that constitutes the width of the surrounding moat. The return journey back is made the same way.

But who can say now that a sloth bear has no sense of affection, no memory and no individual characteristics?

5. How can the reader infer the bear was depressed?

Ⓐ because both the bear and the author's wife cried bitterly while departing
Ⓑ because the bear did not recognize its mistress
Ⓒ because the author's wife was lean and depressed
Ⓓ because Bruno would not eat anything.

Day 3

1. According to the graph, what is the constant of proportionality?

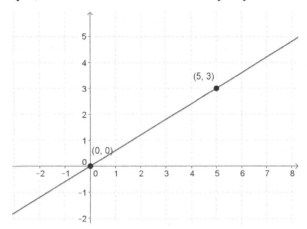

Ⓐ $\dfrac{3}{5}$

Ⓑ 5

Ⓒ 3

Ⓓ $\dfrac{1}{3}$

2. According to the table, how much does one ticket cost?

Number of Tickets	Total Cost
3	$ 21.00
4	$ 28.00
5	$ 35.00
6	$ 42.00

Ⓐ $21.00
Ⓑ $4.75
Ⓒ $7.00
Ⓓ $16.50

3. What is the unit rate for a pound of seed?

Pounds of Seed	Total Cost
10	$ 17.50
20	$ 35.00
30	$ 52.50
40	$ 70.00

Ⓐ $3.50
Ⓑ $1.75
Ⓒ $17.50
Ⓓ $7.25

Day 3

"Bruno the Bear"
Excerpt from *The Bond of Love*

I WILL begin with Bruno; my wife's pet sloth bear. I got him for her by an accident. Two years ago we were passing through the cornfields near a small town in Iowa. People were driving away the wild pigs from the fields by shooting at them. Some were shot and some escaped. We thought that everything was over when suddenly a black sloth bear came out panting in the hot sun.

Now I will not shoot a sloth bear wantonly but unfortunately for the poor beast, one of my companions did not feel the same way about it, and promptly shot the bear on the spot.

As we watched the fallen animal we were surprised to see that the black fur on its back moved and left the prostrate body. Then we saw it was a baby bear that had been riding on its mother's back when the sudden shot had killed her. The little creature ran around its prostrate parent making a pitiful noise.
I ran up to it to attempt a capture. It scooted into the sugarcane field. Following it with my companions, I was at last able to grab it by the scruff of its neck while it snapped and tried to scratch me with its long, hooked claws.

We put it in one of the large jute-bags we had brought and when I got back home I duly presented it to my wife. She was delighted! She at once put a blue colored ribbon around its neck, and after discovering the cub was a 'boy' she christened it Bruno.

Bruno soon took to drinking milk from a bottle. It was but a step further and within a very few days he started eating and drinking everything else. And everything is the right word, for he ate porridge made from any ingredients, vegetables, fruit, nuts, meat (especially pork), curry and rice regardless of condiments and chilies, bread, eggs, chocolates, sweets, pudding, ice-cream, etc., etc., etc. As for drink: milk, tea, coffee, lime juice, aerated water, buttermilk, beer, alcoholic liquor and, in fact, anything liquid. It all went down with relish.

The bear became very attached to our two dogs and to all the children living in and around our farm. He was left quite free in his younger days and spent his time in playing, running into the kitchen and going to sleep in our beds.

One day an accident befell him. I put down poison (barium carbonate) to kill the rats and mice that had got into my library. Bruno entered the library as he often did, and ate some of the poison. Paralysis set in to the extent that he could not stand on his feet. But he dragged himself on his stumps to my wife, who called me. I guessed what had happened.

Off I rushed him in the car to the vet's residence. A case of poisoning! Tame Bear—barium carbonate—what to do? Out came his medical books, and a feverish reference to index began: "What poison did you say, sir?" he asked
"Barium carbonate" I said.

"Ah yes—B—Ba—Barium Salts—Ah! Barium carbonate! Symptoms— paralysis—treatment—injections of . .. Just a minute, sir. I'll bring my syringe and the medicine." Said the doc. I dashed back to the car. Bruno was still floundering about on his stumps, but clearly he was weakening rapidly; there was some vomiting, he was breathing heavily, with heaving flanks and gaping mouth. I was really scared and did not know what to do. I was feeling very guilty and was running in and out of the vet's house doing everything the doc asked me.

"Hold him, everybody!" In goes the hypodermic—Bruno squeals — 10 c.c. of the antidote enters his system without a drop being wasted. Ten minutes later: condition unchanged! Another 10 c.c. Injected! Ten minutes later: breathing less torturous— Bruno can move his arms and legs a little although he cannot stand yet. Thirty minutes later: Bruno gets up and has a great feed! He looks at us disdainfully, as much as to say, 'What's barium carbonate to a big black bear like me?' Bruno was still eating. I was really happy to see him recover.

The months rolled on and Bruno had grown many times the size he was when he came. He had equaled the big dogs in height and had even outgrown them. But was just as sweet, just as mischievous, just as playful. And he was very fond of us all. Above all, he loved my wife, and she loved him too! And he could do a few tricks, too. At the command, 'Bruno, wrestle', or 'Bruno, box,' he vigorously tackled anyone who came forward for a rough and tumble. Give him a stick and say 'Bruno, hold gun', and he pointed the stick at you. Ask him, 'Bruno, where's baby?' and he immediately produced and cradled affectionately a stump of wood which he had carefully concealed in his straw bed. But because of the neighborhoods' and our renters' children, poor Bruno, had to be kept chained most of the time.

Then my son and I advised my wife, and friends advised her too, to give Bruno to the zoo. He was getting too big to keep at home. After some weeks of such advice she at last consented. Hastily, and before she could change her mind, a letter was written to the curator of the zoo. Did he want a tame bear for his collection? He replied, "Yes". The zoo sent a cage in a truck, a distance of hundred – eighty – seven miles, and Bruno was packed off.

We all missed him greatly; but in a sense we were relieved. My wife was inconsolable. She wept and fretted. For the first few days she would not eat a thing. Then she wrote a number of letters to the curator. How was Bruno? Back came the replies,
"Well, but fretting; he refuses food too."

After that, friends visiting the zoo were begged to make a point of seeing how Bruno was getting along. They reported that he was well but looked very thin and sad. All the keepers at the zoo said he was fretting. For three months I managed to restrain my wife from visiting the zoo. Then she said one day, "I must see Bruno. Either you take me by car; or I will go myself by bus or train myself." So I took her by car. Friends had conjectured that the bear would not recognize her. I had thought so too. But while she was yet some yards from his cage Bruno saw her and recognized her. He howled with happiness. She ran up to him, petted him through the bars, and he stood on his head in delight.

For the next three hours she would not leave that cage. She gave him tea, lemonade, cakes, ice cream and what not. Then 'closing time' came and we had to leave. My wife cried bitterly; Bruno cried bitterly; even the hardened curator and the keepers felt depressed. As for me, I had reconciled myself to what I knew was going to happen next.

"Oh please, sir," she asked the curator, "may I have my Bruno back"?
Hesitantly, he answered, "Madam, he belongs to the zoo and is Government property now. I cannot give away Government property. But if my boss, the superintendent agrees, certainly you may have him back."

There followed the return journey home and a visit to the superintendent's office. A tearful pleading: "Bruno and I are both fretting for each other. Will you please give him back to me?" He was a kind-hearted man and consented. Not only that, but he wrote to the curator telling him to lend us a cage for transporting the bear back home.

Back we went to the zoo again, armed with the superintendent's letter. Bruno was driven into a small cage and hoisted on top of the car; the cage was tied securely, and a slow and careful return journey back home was accomplished.

Once home, a squad of workers were engaged for special work around our yard. An island was made for Bruno. It was twenty feet long and fifteen feet wide, and was surrounded by a dry moat, six feet wide and seven feet deep. A wooden box that once housed fowls was brought and put on the island for Bruno to sleep in at night. Straw was placed inside to keep him warm, and his 'baby', the gnarled stump, along with his 'gun', the piece of bamboo, both of which had been sentimentally preserved since he had been sent away to the zoo, were put back for him to play with. In a few days the workers hoisted the cage on to the island and Bruno was released. He was delighted; standing on his hind legs, he pointed his 'gun' and cradled his 'baby'. My wife spent hours sitting on a chair there while he sat on her lap. He was fifteen months old and pretty heavy too!

The way my wife reaches the island and leaves it is interesting. I have tied a rope to the overhanging branch of a maple tree with a loop at its end. Putting one foot in the loop, she kicks off with the other, to bridge the six-foot gap that constitutes the width of the surrounding moat. The return journey back is made the same way.

But who can say now that a sloth bear has no sense of affection, no memory and no individual characteristics?

4. Which of the following would make the best alternate title for this selection?

   Ⓐ **The Pet**
   Ⓑ **Hungry for Love**
   Ⓒ **The Author's Wife**
   Ⓓ **The Animal in the Zoo**

5. What is this story mostly about?

Ⓐ about having a bear as a pet and how to care for it
Ⓑ about the bond that the bear and the author's wife shared
Ⓒ about rescuing a bear
Ⓓ about animals

Represent Proportions by Equations (7.RP.A.2.C)

Day 4

1. 3 hats cost a total of $18. Which equation describes the total cost, C, in terms of the number of hats, n?

   Ⓐ C = 3n
   Ⓑ C = 6n
   Ⓒ C = 0.5n
   Ⓓ 3C = n

2. Use the data in the table to give an equation to represent the proportional relationship.

x	y
0.5	7
1	14
1.5	21
2	28

   Ⓐ y = 14x
   Ⓑ y = 7x
   Ⓒ 7y = x
   Ⓓ 21y = x

3. Kelli has purchased a membership at the gym for the last four months. She has paid the same amount each month, and her total cost so far has been $100. What equation expresses the proportional relationship of the cost and month?

   Ⓐ C = 100m
   Ⓑ C = 50m
   Ⓒ C = 4m
   Ⓓ C = 25m

Day 4

Tryouts

For years, Sam had dreamed of being the best tennis player in the world. He went to tennis practice every single morning, and every single night. He spent every summer at tennis camp, and he gave up long weekends at the beach to work on his game. Now, it seemed his hard work was finally paying off: He was invited to try out for the state tennis team!

Still, there was something that was bothering Sam. The tryouts for the tennis team were on the same day as his mom's birthday, and he knew his family was planning a huge surprise party for her. He didn't want to hurt his mom's feelings by missing the party, but he also didn't want to miss his one shot at being a champion tennis player. He was in a quandary; he didn't know what to do.

For days, Sam went to bed worrying about the decision. If he went to the tryout, he worried he would seem selfish. If he stayed home, he would miss his one big shot at making the state team. In fact, despite the honor of being invited to try out, he hadn't even told his family about the opportunity. He was so stressed about making the decision of whether to go or not that he couldn't even think about sharing the news.

Weeks went by, and Sam was making no progress. Every day his coach asked him if he was ready for the tryout, and Sam couldn't even respond. Finally, Sam couldn't bear the stress any longer. He decided to talk to his grandfather about his predicament.

"You know, your mom wants you to be happy," he told Sam. "It would be a great birthday present for her to know you are making your dream come true."

Sam had never thought of it that way before, and after talking to his grandfather, he knew what he had to do. He immediately went home and sat down with his parents to let them know about the opportunity to try out for the state team. When Sam apologetically told his parents what day the tryouts were, they were so busy shrieking with excitement that he thought maybe they hadn't heard.

"But Mom, that means I'm going to miss your birthday," Sam said. "I am happy you are being so nice about it, but I still feel really bad."
"Are you kidding?" his mom asked? "This is the best present I could ask for!"

4. What is the theme of the above story?

　Ⓐ family values and priorities.
　Ⓑ pleasing everybody in your family
　Ⓒ doing what is very important to you no matter how others feel
　Ⓓ sports above all else

5. What message about relationship is this story trying to pass on to readers?

　Ⓐ Friends can come and go out of each others' lives, but mother's love is permanent
　Ⓑ You should always ask friends to help you with your life choices.
　Ⓒ Open communication helps resolve seemingly difficult problems.
　Ⓓ Thinking over a problem in a quiet place is the best way to resolve a conflict.

Day 5

1. Which point on the graph of the straight line demonstrates that the line represents a proportion?

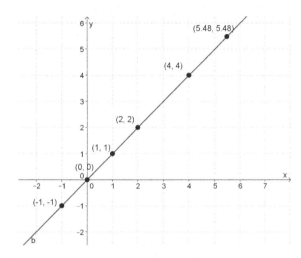

- Ⓐ **(2, 2)**
- Ⓑ **(0, 0)**
- Ⓒ **(5.48, 5.48)**
- Ⓓ **(-1, -1)**

2. Which point on the graph of the straight line names the unit rate of the proportional relationship?

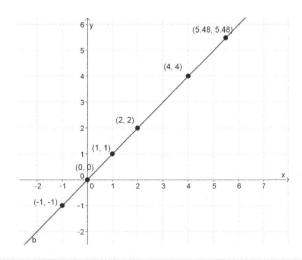

Ⓐ (1, 1)
Ⓑ (0, 0)
Ⓒ (2, 2)
Ⓓ (4, 4)

3. The graph shows the relationship between the number of classes in the school and the total number of students. How many students are there per class?

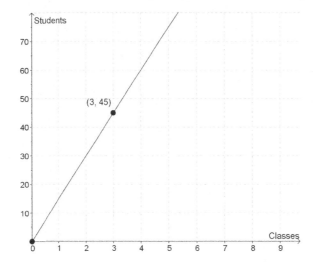

Ⓐ 45 students
Ⓑ 3 students
Ⓒ 135 students
Ⓓ 15 students

Day 5

"The Lament"
by Svern

It is twilight. A thick wet snow is slowly twirling around the newly lighted street lamps and lying in soft thin layers on roofs, on horses' backs, on people's shoulders and hats. The cabdriver, Iona Potapov, is quite white and looks like a phantom: he is bent double as far as a human body can bend double; he is seated on his box; he never makes a move. If a whole snowdrift fell on him, it seems as if he would not find it necessary to shake it off. His little horse is also quite white, and remains motionless; its immobility, its angularity and its straight wooden-looking legs, even close by, give it the appearance of a gingerbread horse worth a kopek. It is, no doubt, plunged in deep thought. If you were snatched from the plough, from your usual gray surroundings, and were thrown into this slough full of monstrous lights, unceasing noise and hurrying people, you too would find it difficult not to think.

Iona and his little horse have not moved from their place for a long while. They left their yard before dinner and, up to now, not a fare. The evening mist is descending over the town, the white lights of the lamps are replacing brighter rays, and the hubbub of the street is getting louder. 'Cabby for Viborg Way!' suddenly hears Iona. 'Cabby!'

Iona jumps and, through his snow-covered eyelashes, sees an officer in a greatcoat, with his hood over his head.
'Viborg way!' the officer repeats. 'Are you asleep, eh? Viborg way!'
With a nod of assent Iona picks up the reins, in consequence of which layers of snow slip off the horse's back and neck. The officer seats himself in the sleigh, the cabdriver smacks his lips to encourage his horse, stretches out his neck like a swan, sits up and, more from habit than necessity, brandishes his whip. The little horse also stretches its neck, bends its wooden-looking legs, and makes a move undecidedly.
'What are you doing, werewolf!' is the exclamation Iona hears from the dark mass moving to and fro, as soon as they have started.

'Where the devil are you going? To the r-r-right!'
'You do not know how to drive. Keep to the right!' calls the officer angrily. A coachman from a private carriage swears at him; a passerby, who has run across the road and rubbed his shoulder

against the horse's nose, looks at him furiously as he sweeps the snow from his sleeve. Iona shifts about on his seat as if he was on needles, moves his elbows as if he were trying to keep his equilibrium, and gasps about like someone suffocating, who does not understand why and wherefore he is there.

'What scoundrels they all are!' jokes the officer; 'one would think they had all entered into an agreement to jostle you or fall under your horse.'

Iona looks around at the officer and moves his lips. He evidently wants to say something but the only sound that issues is a snuffle.

'What?' asks the officer. Iona twists his mouth into a smile and, with an effort, says hoarsely: 'My son, Barin, died this week.' 'Hm! What did he die of?'

Iona turns with his whole body towards his fare and says: 'And who knows! They say high fever. He was three days in the hospital and then died… God's will be done.'

"Turn round! The devil!' sounds from the darkness. 'Have you popped off, old doggie, eh? Use your eyes!'

'Go on, go on,' says the officer, 'otherwise we shall not get there by tomorrow. Hurry up a bit!'

4. What event that occurred before the story begins influences the way the character Iona acts in this story?

   Ⓐ **The death of his son**
   Ⓑ **The winter storm**
   Ⓒ **The officer's harsh comments**
   Ⓓ **Iona's wife's sickness**

5. Based on the plot of this story, what can you assume was The Lament mentioned in the title?

   Ⓐ **The officer had to reach Viborg urgently.**
   Ⓑ **Grief made the cabby confused.**
   Ⓒ **The people were sad because the cabby was not driving carefully.**
   Ⓓ **The horse was lost.**

Week 1 Online Activity

Login to the Lumos student account and complete the following activities.

1. Reading assignment
2. Vocabulary practice
3. Write your summer diary

If you haven't created your Lumos account, use the URL and access code below to get started.

URL: http://www.lumoslearning.com/a/tedbooks

Access Code: G7-8MLSLH-19562

Applying Ratios and Percents (7.RP.A.3)

Day 6

1. What value of x will make these two expressions equivalent?

$$\frac{-3}{7} \text{ and } \frac{x}{21}$$

Ⓐ x = -3
Ⓑ x = 7
Ⓒ x = 9
Ⓓ x = -9

2. If p varies proportionally to s, and $p = 10$ when $s = 2$, which of the following equations correctly models this relationship?

Ⓐ p = 5s
Ⓑ p = 10s
Ⓒ s = 10p
Ⓓ 2s = 10p

3. Solve for x $\frac{72}{108}$ and $\frac{x}{54}$ are equivalent.

Ⓐ x = 18
Ⓑ x = 36
Ⓒ x = 54
Ⓓ x = 24

When and Where? (RL.7.3)

Day 6

"Scouting for Boys"
(Excerpt)

Hi! Stop Thief!" shouted old Blenkinsopp as he rushed out of his little store near the Kaffir village. "He's stolen my sugar. Stop him."

Stop whom? There was nobody in sight running away, "Who stole it?" asked the policeman.

"I don't know, but a whole bag of sugar is missing. It was there only a few minutes ago." A native police tracker was called in and it looked a pretty impossible job for him to single out the tracks of the thief from among dozens of other footprints about the store. However, he presently started off hopefully, at a jog-trot, away out into the bush. In some places he went over hard stony ground but he never checked his pace, although no footmarks could be seen. People wondered how he could possibly find the trail. Still he trotted on. Old Blenkinsopp was feeling the heat and the pace.

At length the tracker suddenly stopped and cast around having evidently lost the trail. Then a grin came on his face as he pointed with his thumb over his shoulder up the tree near which he was standing. There, concealed among the branches, they saw a native with the missing bag of sugar.

How had the tracker spotted him? His sharp eyes had described some grains of sugar sparkling in the dust. The bag leaked, leaving a slight trail of these grains. He followed that trail and when it came to an end in the bush the tracker noticed a string of ants going up a tree. They were after the sugar, and so was he, and between them they brought about the capture of the thief.

Old Blenkinsopp was so pleased that he promptly opened the bag and spilled a lot of the sugar on the ground as a reward to the ants.

I expect that he also patted the tracker on the back for his cleverness in using his eyes to see the grains of sugar and the ants, and in using his wits to see why the ants were climbing the tree.

4. Based on the details in this story, where can you infer where the story begins (setting)?

Ⓐ a store
Ⓑ a house
Ⓒ a bakery
Ⓓ a police station

"The Lament"
by Srvani

It is twilight. A thick wet snow is slowly twirling around the newly lighted street lamps and lying in soft thin layers on roofs, on horses' backs, on people's shoulders and hats. The cabdriver, Iona Potapov, is quite white and looks like a phantom: he is bent double as far as a human body can bend double; he is seated on his box; he never makes a move. If a whole snowdrift fell on him, it seems as if he would not find it necessary to shake it off. His little horse is also quite white, and remains motionless; its immobility, its angularity and its straight wooden-looking legs, even close by, give it the appearance of a gingerbread horse worth a kopek. It is, no doubt, plunged in deep thought. If you were snatched from the plough, from your usual gray surroundings, and were thrown into this slough full of monstrous lights, unceasing noise and hurrying people, you too would find it difficult not to think.

Iona and his little horse have not moved from their place for a long while. They left their yard before dinner and, up to now, not a fare. The evening mist is descending over the town, the white lights of the lamps are replacing brighter rays, and the hubbub of the street is getting louder.
'Cabby for Viborg Way!' suddenly hears Iona. 'Cabby!'
Iona jumps and, through his snow-covered eyelashes, sees an officer in a greatcoat, with his hood over his head.
'Viborg way!' the officer repeats. 'Are you asleep, eh? Viborg way!'
With a nod of assent Iona picks up the reins, in consequence of which layers of snow slip off the horse's back and neck. The officer seats himself in the sleigh, the cabdriver smacks his lips to encourage his horse, stretches out his neck like a swan, sits up and, more from habit than necessity, brandishes his whip. The little horse also stretches its neck, bends its wooden-looking legs, and makes a move undecidedly.

'What are you doing, werewolf!' is the exclamation Iona hears from the dark mass moving to and fro, as soon as they have started.
'Where the devil are you going? To the r-r-right!'
'You do not know how to drive. Keep to the right!' calls the officer angrily. A coachman from a private carriage swears at him; a passerby, who has run across the road and rubbed his shoulder against the horse's nose, looks at him furiously as he sweeps the snow from his sleeve. Iona shifts about on his seat as if he was on needles, moves his elbows as if he were trying to keep his equilibrium, and gasps about like someone suffocating, who does not understand why and wherefore he is there.

'What scoundrels they all are!' jokes the officer; 'one would think they had all entered into an agreement to jostle you or fall under your horse.'

Iona looks around at the officer and moves his lips. He evidently wants to say something but the only sound that issues is a snuffle.

'What?' asks the officer.

Iona twists his mouth into a smile and, with an effort, says hoarsely: 'My son, Barin, died this week.' '

Hm! What did he die of?'

Iona turns with his whole body towards his fare and says: 'And who knows! They say high fever. He was three

days in the hospital and then died… God's will be done.'

"Turn round! The devil!' sounds from the darkness. 'Have you popped off, old doggie, eh? Use your eyes!'

'Go on, go on,' says the officer, 'otherwise we shall not get there by tomorrow. Hurry up a bit!'

5. Which detail in the above passage tells us this story is set in the winter?

Ⓐ **It is twilight.**

Ⓑ **His little horse is also quite white, and remains motionless;**

Ⓒ **A thick wet snow is slowly twirling around the newly lighted street lamps and lying in soft thin layers on roofs, on horses' backs, on people's shoulders and hats.**

Ⓓ **The cabdriver, Iona Potapov, is quite white and looks like a phantom: he is bent double as far as a human body can bend double;**

Day 7

1. Which picture represents the rational number $\frac{1}{2}$?

    Ⓐ

    Ⓑ

    Ⓒ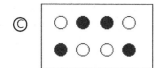

    Ⓓ

2. Evaluate: 25 + 2.005 - 7.253 - 2.977
    - Ⓐ -16.775
    - Ⓑ 16.775
    - Ⓒ 167.75
    - Ⓓ 1.6775

3. Add and/or subtract as indicated : $-3\dfrac{4}{5} + 9\dfrac{7}{10} - 2\dfrac{11}{20} =$

(A) $3\dfrac{7}{20}$

(B) $4\dfrac{7}{10}$

(C) $4\dfrac{9}{20}$

(D) $3\dfrac{1}{20}$

Day 7

"Bruno the Bear"
From *A Bond of Love*

I WILL begin with Bruno; my wife's pet sloth bear. I got him for her by an accident. Two years ago we were passing through the cornfields near a small town in Iowa. People were driving away the wild pigs from the fields by shooting at them. Some were shot and some escaped. We thought that everything was over when suddenly a black sloth bear came out panting in the hot sun.

Now I will not shoot a sloth bear wantonly but unfortunately for the poor beast, one of my companions did not feel the same way about it, and promptly shot the bear on the spot.

As we watched the fallen animal we were surprised to see that the black fur on its back moved and left the prostrate body. Then we saw it was a baby bear that had been riding on its mother's back when the sudden shot had killed her. The little creature ran around its prostrate parent making a pitiful noise.

I ran up to it to attempt a capture. It scooted into the sugarcane field. Following it with my companions, I was at last able to grab it by the scruff of its neck while it snapped and tried to scratch me with its long, hooked claws. We put it in one of the large jute-bags we had brought and when I got back home I duly presented it to my wife. She was delighted! She at once put a blue colored ribbon around its neck, and after discovering the cub was a 'boy' she christened it Bruno.

Bruno soon took to drinking milk from a bottle. It was but a step further and within a very few days he started eating and drinking everything else. And everything is the right word, for he ate porridge made from any ingredients, vegetables, fruit, nuts, meat (especially pork), curry and rice regardless of condiments and chilies, bread, eggs, chocolates, sweets, pudding, ice-cream, etc., etc., etc. As for drink: milk, tea, coffee, lime juice, aerated water, buttermilk, beer, alcoholic liquor and, in fact, anything liquid. It all went down with relish.

The bear became very attached to our two dogs and to all the children living in and around our farm. He was left quite free in his younger days and spent his time in playing, running into the kitchen and going to sleep in our beds.

One day an accident befell him. I put down poison (barium carbonate) to kill the rats and mice that had got into my library. Bruno entered the library as he often did, and ate some of the poison.

Paralysis set in to the extent that he could not stand on his feet. But he dragged himself on his stumps to my wife, who called me. I guessed what had happened. Off I rushed him in the car to the vet's residence. A case of poisoning! Tame Bear—barium carbonate—what to do?

Out came his medical books, and a feverish reference to index began: "What poison did you say, sir?" he asked
"Barium carbonate" I said.

"Ah yes—B—Ba—Barium Salts—Ah! Barium carbonate! Symptoms— paralysis—treatment—injections of . .. Just a minute, sir. I'll bring my syringe and the medicine." Said the doc. I dashed back to the car. Bruno was still floundering about on his stumps, but clearly he was weakening rapidly; there was some vomiting, he was breathing heavily, with heaving flanks and gaping mouth. I was really scared and did not know what to do. I was feeling very guilty and was running in and out of the vet's house doing everything the doc asked me.

Hold him, everybody! In goes the hypodermic—Bruno squeals — 10 c.c. of the antidote enters his system without a drop being wasted. Ten minutes later: condition unchanged! Another 10 c.c. Injected! Ten minutes later: breathing less torturous— Bruno can move his arms and legs a little although he cannot stand yet. Thirty minutes later: Bruno gets up and has a great feed! He looks at us disdainfully, as much as to say, 'What's barium carbonate to a big black bear like me?' Bruno was still eating. I was really happy to see him recover.

The months rolled on and Bruno had grown many times the size he was when he came. He had equaled the big dogs in height and had even outgrown them. But was just as sweet, just as mischievous, just as playful. And he was very fond of us all. Above all, he loved my wife, and she loved him too! And he could do a few tricks, too. At the command, 'Bruno, wrestle', or 'Bruno, box,' he vigorously tackled anyone who came forward for a rough and tumble. Give him a stick and say 'Bruno, hold gun', and he pointed the stick at you. Ask him, 'Bruno, where's baby?' and he immediately produced and cradled affectionately a stump of wood which he had carefully concealed in his straw bed. But because of the neighborhoods' and our renters' children, poor Bruno, had to be kept chained most of the time.

Then my son and I advised my wife, and friends advised her too, to give Bruno to the zoo. He was getting too big to keep at home. After some weeks of such advice she at last consented. Hastily, and before she could change her mind, a letter was written to the curator of the zoo. Did he want a tame bear for his collection? He replied, "Yes". The zoo sent a cage in a truck, a distance of hundred – eighty – seven miles, and Bruno was packed off.

We all missed him greatly; but in a sense we were relieved. My wife was inconsolable. She wept and fretted. For the first few days she would not eat a thing. Then she wrote a number of letters to the curator. How was Bruno? Back came the replies,
"Well, but fretting; he refuses food too."

After that, friends visiting the zoo were begged to make a point of seeing how Bruno was getting along. They reported that he was well but looked very thin and sad. All the keepers at the zoo said he was fretting. For three months I managed to restrain my wife from visiting the zoo.

Then she said one day, "I must see Bruno. Either you take me by car; or I will go myself by bus or train myself." So I took her by car.

Friends had conjectured that the bear would not recognize her. I had thought so too. But while she was yet some yards from his cage Bruno saw her and recognized her. He howled with happiness. She ran up to him, petted him through the bars, and he stood on his head in delight.

For the next three hours she would not leave that cage. She gave him tea, lemonade, cakes, ice cream and what not. Then 'closing time' came and we had to leave. My wife cried bitterly; Bruno cried bitterly; even the hardened curator and the keepers felt depressed. As for me, I had reconciled myself to what I knew was going to happen next.
"Oh please, sir," she asked the curator, "may I have my Bruno back"?
Hesitantly, he answered, "Madam, he belongs to the zoo and is Government property now. I cannot give away Government property. But if my boss, the superintendent agrees, certainly you may have him back."
There followed the return journey home and a visit to the superintendent's office.

A tearful pleading: "Bruno and I are both fretting for each other. Will you please give him back to me?" He was a kind-hearted man and consented. Not only that, but he wrote to the curator telling him to lend us a cage for transporting the bear back home.
Back we went to the zoo again, armed with the superintendent's letter. Bruno was driven into a small cage and hoisted on top of the car; the cage was tied securely, and a slow and careful return journey back home was accomplished.

Once home, a squad of workers were engaged for special work around our yard. An island was made for Bruno. It was twenty feet long and fifteen feet wide, and was surrounded by a dry moat, six feet wide and seven feet deep. A wooden box that once housed fowls was brought and put on the island for Bruno to sleep in at night. Straw was placed inside to keep him warm, and his 'baby', the gnarled stump, along with his 'gun', the piece of bamboo, both of which had been sentimentally preserved since he had been sent away to the zoo, were put back for him to play with.

In a few days the workers hoisted the cage on to the island and Bruno was released. He was delighted; standing on his hind legs, he pointed his 'gun' and cradled his 'baby'. My wife spent hours sitting on a chair there while he sat on her lap. He was fifteen months old and pretty heavy too!

The way my wife reaches the island and leaves it is interesting. I have tied a rope to the overhanging branch of a maple tree with a loop at its end. Putting one foot in the loop, she kicks off with the other, to bridge the six-foot gap that constitutes the width of the surrounding moat. The return journey back is made the same way.

But who can say now that a sloth bear has no sense of affection, no memory and no individual characteristics?

4. What motivated the narrator to keep Bruno chained up?

Ⓐ **because he had grown big**
Ⓑ **because he was very playful and this scared some of the children in the neighbor hood**
Ⓒ **because he was very dangerous**
Ⓓ **because he was a bear**

Best Friends to Boyfriend/Girlfriend

Ever since they were kids, Julie and Max had been best friends. They went to kindergarten together. They went to summer camp together, They hung out together every weekend. But suddenly, things between the two had started to change.

Max started playing on the football team and didn't have much time for Julie anymore. He was always busy, and he never seemed to make it to study hall, where the two used to swap stories about their favorite (or least favorite) teachers. In class, Julie noticed that Max never seemed to have his homework done on time anymore. She even noticed that he got a D on his last paper. She knew something was going on with him – but what?

At first, Julie decided to play it cool and see how things went. She tried waiting in the hall for Max after class to see if she could ask if he was OK. But days went by, and he never had time to stop. He'd rush right past her in the hall, only to leave her feeling even worse about what was happening between them.

Even though she wasn't sure she could handle the situation herself, Julie didn't want to talk to her parents because she was afraid they would tell her not to hang out with Max anymore. She barely saw him as it was, so she knew it would just make things worse if her parents didn't approve of him. She didn't want to tell Max's parents either because she didn't want him to get in trouble. Still, it seemed like something needed to change.

Julie decided to go to one of her school counselors and let her know she was concerned. When she walked into Mrs. Smith's room, she was surprised to see that Max was already sitting there.

"I'm sorry, I'll come back," Julie said.
"No, stay," said Max. "Maybe you can help."

Julie was surprised to find that Max had visited the counselor's office for the same reason she had: he was starting to feel overwhelmed with all of the things he was supposed to be doing as a student, an athlete and a friend. He needed some guidance on how to determine what truly mattered, and how to divide his time between all of the things that were important to him.

When she realized that Max was still the same old Max (just a little more stressed), Julie was relieved. She was also happy to know that he had come to the conclusion on his own, without her having to talk to someone else about it. She decided it was a sign they were both growing up.

http://www.fanfiction.net/s/5080637/6/Best-Friends-to-BoyfriendGirlfriend

5. What events in the story did NOT contribute to the character of Max being overwhelmed?

- Ⓐ work commitments
- Ⓑ school commitments
- Ⓒ sports commitments
- Ⓓ parent's expectations

Add and Subtract Rational Numbers (7.NS.A.1.B)

1. If p + q has a value that is exactly 1/3 less than p, what is the value of q?

   (A) –1/3
   (B) 2/5
   (C) 1/3
   (D) –2/5

2. What is the sum of k and the opposite of k?

   (A) 2k
   (B) k + 1
   (C) 0
   (D) –1

3. If p + q has a value of 12/5, and p has a value of 4/5, what is the value of q?

   (A) 5/8
   (B) 8/5
   (C) 1/3
   (D) 3/2

Day 8

From THE HISTORY OF THE SEVEN FAMILIES OF THE LAKE PIPPLE-POPPLE.
by Edward Lear

The Parrots lived upon the Soffsky-Poffsky trees, which were beautiful to behold, and covered with blue leaves; and they fed upon fruit, artichokes, and striped beetles.

The Storks walked in and out of the Lake Pipple-Popple, and ate frogs for breakfast, and buttered toast for tea; but on account of the extreme length of their legs they could not sit down, and so they walked about continually. The Geese, having webs to their feet, caught quantities of flies, which they ate for dinner.

The Owls anxiously looked after mice, which they caught, and made into sago-puddings. The Guinea Pigs toddled about the gardens, and ate lettuces and Cheshire cheese.

The Cats sate still in the sunshine, and fed upon sponge biscuits. The Fishes lived in the lake, and fed chiefly on boiled periwinkles. And all these seven families lived together in the utmost fun and felicity.

4. How do the author's descriptions of the animals' habitats affect the tone of the story?

Ⓐ They make the animals appear hungry all the time.
Ⓑ They make the animals seem greedy.
Ⓒ They create a tone of nonsense and silliness.
Ⓓ They show how diverse the animals are.

THE WONDERFUL HAIR by A. H. Wraitslaw

There was a man who was very poor, but so well supplied with children that he was utterly unable to maintain them, and one morning more than once prepared to kill them, in order not to see their misery in dying of hunger, but his wife prevented him. One night a child came to him in his sleep, and said to him: "Man! I see that you are making up your mind to destroy and to kill your poor little children, and I know that you are distressed there at; but in the morning you will find under your pillow a mirror, a red kerchief, and an embroidered pocket-handkerchief; take all three secretly and tell nobody; then go to such a hill; by it you will find a stream; go along it

till you come to its fountain-head; there you will find a damsel as bright as the sun, with her hair hanging down over her back. Be on your guard, that the ferocious she-dragon do not coil round you; do not converse with her if she speaks; for if you converse with her, she will poison you, and turn you into a fish or something else, and will then devour you but if she bids you examine her head, examine it, and as you turn over her hair, look, and you will find one hair as red as blood; pull it out and run back again; then, if she suspects and begins to run after you, throw her first the embroidered pocket-handkerchief, then the kerchief, and, lastly, the mirror; then she will find occupation for herself. And sell that hair to some rich man; but don't let them cheat you, for that hair is worth countless wealth; and you will thus enrich yourself and maintain your children."

When the poor man awoke, he found everything under his pillow, just as the child had told him in his sleep; and then he went to the hill. When there, he found the stream, went on and on along-side of it, till he came to the fountain-head. Having looked about him to see where the damsel was, he espied her above a piece of water, like sunbeams threaded on a needle, and she was embroidering at a frame on stuff, the threads of which were young men's hair. As soon as he saw her, he made a reverence to her, and she stood on her feet and questioned him: "Whence are you, unknown young man?" But he held his tongue. She questioned him again: "Who are you? Why have you come?" and much else of all sorts; but he was as mute as a stone, making signs with his hands, as if he were deaf and wanted help. Then she told him to sit down on her skirt. He did not wait for any more orders, but sat down, and she bent down her head to him, that he might examine it. Turning over the hair of her head, as if to examine it, he was not long in finding that red hair, and separated it from the other hair, pulled it out, jumped off her skirt and ran away back as he best could. She noticed it, and ran at his heels full speed after him. He looked round, and seeing that she was about to overtake him, threw, as he was told, the embroidered pocket-handkerchief on the way, and when she saw the pocket-handkerchief she stooped and began to overhaul it in every direction, admiring the embroidery, till he had got a good way off. Then the damsel placed the pocket-handkerchief in her bosom, and ran after him again. When he saw that she was about to overtake him, he threw the red kerchief, and she again occupied herself, admiring and gazing, till the poor man had again got a good way off. Then the damsel became exasperated, and threw both the pocket-handkerchief and the kerchief on the way, and ran after him in pursuit. Again, when he saw that she was about to overtake him, he threw the mirror. When the damsel came to the mirror, the like of which she had never seen before, she lifted it up, and when she saw herself in it, not knowing that it was herself, but thinking that it was somebody else, she, as it were, fell in love with herself in the mirror, and the man got so far off that she was no longer able to overtake him. When she saw that she could not catch him, she turned back, and the man reached his home safe and sound. After arriving at his home, he showed his wife the hair, and told her all that had happened to him, but she began to jeer and laugh at him. But he paid no attention to her, and went to a town to sell the hair. A crowd of all sorts of people and merchants collected round him; one offered a sequin, another two, and so on, higher and higher, till they came to a hundred gold sequins. Just then the emperor heard of the hair, summoned the man into his presence, and said to him that he would give him a thousand sequins for it, and he sold it to him. What was the hair? The emperor split it in two from top to bottom, and found registered in it in writing many remarkable things, which happened in the olden time since the beginning of the world. Thus the man became rich and lived on with his wife and children. And that child, that came to him in his sleep, was an angel sent by the Lord God, whose will it was to aid the poor man, and to reveal secrets which had not been revealed till then.

5. What is the tone at the end of this story?

Ⓐ Serious
Ⓑ Joyful
Ⓒ Angry
Ⓓ Confused

Additive Inverse and Distance Between Two Points on a Number Line (7.NS.A.1.C)

Day 9

1. Which of the following is the same as 7 − (3 + 4)?

    Ⓐ 7 + (−3) + (−4)
    Ⓑ 7 +(−3 + 4)
    Ⓒ 7 + 7
    Ⓓ −7 − 7

2. Which of the following expressions represents the distance between the two points?

    Ⓐ |4-3|
    Ⓑ (-3)-4
    Ⓒ |(-3)-4|
    Ⓓ 4-3

3. Kyle and Mark started at the same location. Kyle traveled 5 miles due east, while Mark traveled 3 miles due West. How far apart are they?

    Ⓐ 2 miles
    Ⓑ 8 miles
    Ⓒ 15 miles
    Ⓓ 12 miles

Day 9

"Do Not Go Gentle into that Good Night"
Dylan Thomas

Do not go gentle into that good night,
Old age should burn and rave at close of day;
Rage, rage against the dying of the light.
Though wise men at their end know dark is right,
Because their words had forked no lightning they
Do not go gentle into that good night.
Good men, the last wave by, crying how bright
Their frail deeds might have danced in a green bay,
Rage, rage against the dying of the light.
Wild men who caught and sang the sun in flight,
And learn, too late, they grieved it on its way,
Do not go gentle into that good night.
Grave men, near death, who see with blinding sight
Blind eyes could blaze like meteors and be gay,
Rage, rage against the dying of the light.
And you, my father, there on the sad height,
Curse, bless me now with your fierce tears, I pray.
Do not go gentle into that good night.
Rage, rage against the dying of the light.

4. **Which characteristic of this poem indicates it is a villanelle?**

   Ⓐ **There are two rhyming patterns.**
   Ⓑ **The poem is written in iambic meter.**
   Ⓒ **The subject of the poem is death.**
   Ⓓ **There is a chorus or refrain between every two stanzas.**

5. **Which answer does not use repetition to develop the tone of this poem?**

   Ⓐ **The word rage is repeated to develop the idea that one can fight back against death.**
   Ⓑ **The word men is repeated to remind the subject about whom he is writing.**
   Ⓒ **The word gentle is repeated to remind the reader how to behave.**
   Ⓓ **The word me is repeated to establish the focus of the poem.**

Strategies for Adding and Subtracting Rational Numbers (7.NS.A.1.D)

Day 10

1. What property is illustrated in the equation?:

    $7 + \dfrac{1}{2} = \dfrac{1}{2} + 7$

    - Ⓐ Commutative property of addition
    - Ⓑ Associate property of addition
    - Ⓒ Distributive property
    - Ⓓ Identity property of addition

2. Which is a valid use of properties to make the expression easier to calculate?

    $92 - 8 = ?$

    - Ⓐ $90 - 2 - 8$
    - Ⓑ $82 - (10 - 8)$
    - Ⓒ $82 + (10 - 8)$
    - Ⓓ $(80 + 2) - 8$

3. Find the sum of the mixed numbers.

    $4\dfrac{7}{8} + 7\dfrac{5}{8}$

    - Ⓐ $11\dfrac{5}{8}$
    - Ⓑ $12\dfrac{1}{2}$
    - Ⓒ $12\dfrac{7}{8}$
    - Ⓓ $11\dfrac{1}{2}$

THE EMPEROR'S NEW CLOTHES
by: Hans Christian Anderson

Many years ago there was an Emperor, who was so excessively fond of new clothes that he spent all his money on them. He cared nothing about his soldiers, nor for the theatre, nor for driving in the woods except for the sake of showing off his new clothes. He had a costume for every hour in the day, and instead of saying, as one does about any other king or emperor, 'He is in his council chamber,' here one always said, 'The Emperor is in his dressing-room.'

Life was very gay in the great town where he lived; hosts of strangers came to visit it every day, and among them one day two swindlers. They gave themselves out as weavers, and said that they knew how to weave the most beautiful stuffs imaginable. Not only were the colours and patterns unusually fine, but the clothes that were made of the stuffs had the peculiar quality of becoming invisible to every person who was not fit for the office he held, or if he was impossibly dull.

Those must be splendid clothes,' thought the Emperor. 'By wearing them I should be able to discover which men in my kingdom are unfitted for their posts. I shall distinguish the wise men from the fools. Yes, I certainly must order some of that stuff to be woven for me.

He paid the two swindlers a lot of money in advance so that they might begin their work at once.

They did put up two looms and pretended to weave, but they had nothing whatever upon their shuttles. At the outset they asked for a quantity of the finest silk and the purest gold thread, all of which they put into their own bags, while they worked away at the empty looms far into the night. I should like to know how those weavers are getting on with the stuff,' thought the Emperor; but he felt a little queer when he reflected that anyone who was stupid or unfit for his post would not be able to see it. He certainly thought that he need have no fears for himself, but still he thought he would send somebody else first to see how it was getting on. Everybody in the town knew what wonderful power the stuff possessed, and everyone was anxious to see how stupid his neighbour was.

I will send my faithful old minister to the weavers,' thought the Emperor. 'He will be best able to see how the stuff looks, for he is a clever man, and no one fulfils his duties better than he does!'

So the good old minister went into the room where the two swindlers sat working at the empty loom.

Heaven preserve us!' thought the old minister, opening his eyes very wide. 'Why, I can't see a thing!' But he took care not to say so.
Both the swindlers begged him to be good enough to step a little nearer, and asked if he did not think it a good pattern and beautiful colouring. They pointed to the empty loom, and the poor old minister stared as hard as he could, but he could not see anything, for of course there was nothing to see.
Good heavens!' thought he, 'is it possible that I am a fool. I have never thought so, and nobody must know it. Am I not fit for my post? It will never do to say that I cannot see the stuffs.

Well, sir, you don't say anything about the stuff,' said the one who was pretending to weave.

Oh, it is beautiful! quite charming!' said the old minister, looking through his spectacles; 'this pattern and these colours! I will certainly tell the Emperor that the stuff pleases me very much.

We are delighted to hear you say so,' said the swindlers, and then they named all the colours and described the peculiar pattern. The old minister paid great attention to what they said, so as to be able to repeat it when he got home to the Emperor.

Then the swindlers went on to demand more money, more silk, and more gold, to be able to proceed with the weaving; but they put it all into their own pockets—not a single strand was ever put into the loom, but they went on as before weaving at the empty loom.

The Emperor soon sent another faithful official to see how the stuff was getting on, and if it would soon be ready. The same thing happened to him as to the minister; he looked and looked, but as there was only the empty loom, he could see nothing at all.

Is not this a beautiful piece of stuff?' said both the swindlers, showing and explaining the beautiful pattern and colours which were not there to be seen.

I know I am not a fool!' thought the man, 'so it must be that I am unfit for my good post! It is very strange, though! However, one must not let it appear!' So he praised the stuff he did not see, and assured them of his delight in the beautiful colours and the originality of the design. 'It is absolutely charming!' he said to the Emperor. Everybody in the town was talking about this splendid stuff.

Now the Emperor thought he would like to see it while it was still on the loom. So, accompanied by a number of selected courtiers, among whom were the two faithful officials who had already seen the imaginary stuff, he went to visit the crafty impostors, who were working away as hard as ever they could at the empty loom.

It is magnificent!' said both the honest officials. 'Only see, your Majesty, what a design! What colours!' And they pointed to the empty loom, for they thought no doubt the others could see the stuff.

What!' thought the Emperor; 'I see nothing at all! This is terrible! Am I a fool? Am I not fit to be Emperor? Why, nothing worse could happen to me!
Oh, it is beautiful!' said the Emperor. 'It has my highest approval!' and he nodded his satisfaction as he gazed at the empty loom. Nothing would induce him to say that he could not see anything.

The whole suite gazed and gazed, but saw nothing more than all the others. However, they all exclaimed with his Majesty, 'It is very beautiful!' and they advised him to wear a suit made of this wonderful cloth on the occasion of a great procession which was just about to take place. 'It is magnificent!
gorgeous! excellent!' went from mouth to mouth; they were all equally delighted with it.

The Emperor gave each of the rogues an order of knighthood to be worn in their buttonholes and the title of 'Gentlemen weavers.'

The swindlers sat up the whole night, before the day on which the procession was to take place, burning sixteen candles; so that people might see how anxious they were to get the Emperor's new clothes ready. They pretended to take the stuff off the loom. They cut it out in the air with a huge pair of scissors, and they stitched away with needles without any thread in them. At last they said: 'Now the Emperor's new clothes are ready!
The Emperor, with his grandest courtiers, went to them himself, and both the swindlers raised one arm in the air, as if they were holding something, and said: 'See, these are the trousers, this is the coat, here is the mantle!' and so on. 'It is as light as a spider's web. One might think one had nothing on, but that is the very beauty of it!'

Yes!' said all the courtiers, but they could not see anything, for there was nothing to see.

Will your imperial majesty be graciously pleased to take off your clothes,' said, the impostors, 'so that we may put on the new ones, along here before the great mirror?'
The Emperor took off all his clothes, and the impostors pretended to give him one article of dress after the other of the new ones which they had pretended to make. They pretended to fasten something round his waist and to tie on something; this was the train, and the Emperor turned round and round in front of the mirror.

How well his majesty looks in the new clothes! How becoming they are!' cried all the people

round. 'What a design, and what colours! They are most gorgeous robes!'
The canopy is waiting outside which is to be carried over your majesty in the procession,' said the master of the ceremonies.

Well, I am quite ready,' said the Emperor. 'Don't the clothes fit well?' and then he turned round again in front of the mirror, so that he should seem to be looking at his grand things.

The chamberlains who were to carry the train stooped and pretended to lift it from the ground with both hands, and they walked along with their hands in the air. They dared not let it appear that they could not see anything.
Then the Emperor walked along in the procession under the gorgeous canopy, and everybody in the streets and at the windows exclaimed, 'How beautiful the Emperor's new clothes are! What a splendid train! And they fit to perfection!' Nobody would let it appear that he could see nothing, for then he would not be fit for his post, or else he was a fool.
None of the Emperor's clothes had been so successful before.
But he has got nothing on,' said a little child.

Oh, listen to the innocent,' said its father; and one person whispered to the other what the child had said. 'He has nothing on; a child says he has nothing on!

But he has nothing on!' at last cried all the people.
The Emperor writhed, for he knew it was true, but he thought 'the procession must go on now,' so held himself stiffer than ever, and the chamberlains held up the invisible train.

4. Which excerpt from the text provides the reason the Emperor agreed to buy clothes from the swindlers?

Ⓐ Not only were the colors and patterns unusually fine, but the clothes that were made of the stuffs had the peculiar quality of becoming invisible to every person who was not fit for the office he held, or if he was impossibly dull.

Ⓑ Life was very gay in the great town where he lived; hosts of strangers came to visit it every day, and among them one day two swindlers. They gave themselves out as weavers, and said that they knew how to weave the most beautiful stuffs imaginable.

Ⓒ At the outset they asked for a quantity of the finest silk and the purest gold thread, all of which they put into their own bags, while they worked away at the empty looms far into the night.

Ⓓ 'I know I am not a fool!' thought the man, 'so it must be that I am unfit for my good post! It is very strange, though! However, one must not let it appear!' So he praised the stuff he did not see, and assured them of his delight in the beautiful colors and the originality of the design.

5. What character trait do the Emperor and his minister share?

Ⓐ They are both insecure about their qualifications.
Ⓑ They both want to fool the public
Ⓒ They both want the Emperor to have the most wonderful clothing available.
Ⓓ Both men are able to imagine things that are not visible.

Week 2 Online Activity

Login to the Lumos student account and complete the following activities.

1. Reading assignment
2. Vocabulary practice
3. Write your summer diary

If you haven't created your Lumos account, use the URL and access code below to get started.

URL: http://www.lumoslearning.com/a/tedbooks

Access Code: G7-8MLSLH-19562

Rational Numbers, Multiplication and Division (7.NS.A.2.A)

1. Fill in the blank to make a true equation.

   (-9)(___) = 36

   - Ⓐ - 4
   - Ⓑ   4
   - Ⓒ   6
   - Ⓓ - 6

2. Evaluate the following expression.

   - 2(a + 3b) =

   - Ⓐ - 2a + 3b
   - Ⓑ - 2a - 3b
   - Ⓒ - 2a + 6b
   - Ⓓ - 2a - 6b

3. Simplify the following complex fraction.

   $$\frac{\frac{1}{2}}{\frac{2}{3}}$$

   - Ⓐ $\dfrac{4}{3}$

   - Ⓑ $\dfrac{1}{2}$

   - Ⓒ $\dfrac{3}{4}$

   - Ⓓ $\dfrac{4}{3}$

Day 11 — Finding Patterns – Comparing and Contrasting (RL.7.7)

THE WONDERFUL HAIR by A. H. Wraitslaw

There was a man who was very poor, but so well supplied with children that he was utterly unable to maintain them, and one morning more than once prepared to kill them, in order not to see their misery in dying of hunger, but his wife prevented him. One night a child came to him in his sleep, and said to him: "Man! I see that you are making up your mind to destroy and to kill your poor little children, and I know that you are distressed there at; but in the morning you will find under your pillow a mirror, a red kerchief, and an embroidered pocket-handkerchief; take all three secretly and tell nobody; then go to such a hill; by it you will find a stream; go along it till you come to its fountain-head; there you will find a damsel as bright as the sun, with her hair hanging down over her back. Be on your guard, that the ferocious she-dragon do not coil round you; do not converse with her if she speaks; for if you converse with her, she will poison you, and turn you into a fish or something else, and will then devour you but if she bids you examine her head, examine it, and as you turn over her hair, look, and you will find one hair as red as blood; pull it out and run back again; then, if she suspects and begins to run after you, throw her first the embroidered pocket-handkerchief, then the kerchief, and, lastly, the mirror; then she will find occupation for herself. And sell that hair to some rich man; but don't let them cheat you, for that hair is worth countless wealth; and you will thus enrich yourself and maintain your children."

When the poor man awoke, he found everything under his pillow, just as the child had told him in his sleep; and then he went to the hill. When there, he found the stream, went on and on alongside of it, till he came to the fountain-head. Having looked about him to see where the damsel was, he espied her above a piece of water, like sunbeams threaded on a needle, and she was embroidering at a frame on stuff, the threads of which were young men's hair. As soon as he saw her, he made a reverence to her, and she stood on her feet and questioned him: "Whence are you, unknown young man?" But he held his tongue. She questioned him again: "Who are you? Why have you come?" and much else of all sorts; but he was as mute as a stone, making signs with his hands, as if he were deaf and wanted help. Then she told him to sit down on her skirt. He did not wait for any more orders, but sat down, and she bent down her head to him, that he might examine it. Turning over the hair of her head, as if to examine it, he was not long in finding that red hair, and separated it from the other hair, pulled it out, jumped off her skirt and ran away back as he best could. She noticed it, and ran at his heels full speed after him. He looked round, and seeing that she was about to overtake him, threw, as he was told, the embroidered pocket-handkerchief on the way, and when she saw the pocket-handkerchief she stooped and began to overhaul it in every direction, admiring the embroidery, till he had got a good way off. Then the damsel placed the pocket-handkerchief in her bosom, and ran after him again.

When he saw that she was about to overtake him, he threw the red kerchief, and she again occupied herself, admiring and gazing, till the poor man had again got a good way off. Then the damsel became exasperated, and threw both the pocket-handkerchief and the kerchief on the way, and ran after him in pursuit. Again, when he saw that she was about to overtake him, he threw the mirror. When the damsel came to the mirror, the like of which she had never seen before, she lifted it up, and when she saw herself in it, not knowing that it was herself, but thinking that it was somebody else, she, as it were, fell in love with herself in the mirror, and the man got so far off that she was no longer able to overtake him. When she saw that she could not catch him, she turned back, and the man reached his home safe and sound. After arriving at his home, he showed his wife the hair, and told her all that had happened to him, but she began to jeer and laugh at him.

But he paid no attention to her, and went to a town to sell the hair. A crowd of all sorts of people and merchants collected round him; one offered a sequin, another two, and so on, higher and higher, till they came to a hundred gold sequins. Just then the emperor heard of the hair, summoned the man into his presence, and said to him that he would give him a thousand sequins for it, and he sold it to him. What was the hair? The emperor split it in two from top to bottom, and found registered in it in writing many remarkable things, which happened in the olden time since the beginning of the world. Thus the man became rich and lived on with his wife and children. And that child, that came to him in his sleep, was an angel sent by the Lord God, whose will it was to aid the poor man, and to reveal secrets which had not been revealed till then.

4. How is the outcome of this selection different than what the little boy predicted when he spoke to his father through a dream?

Ⓐ The father is not able to earn a great deal of money by selling the damsel's hair.
Ⓑ The damsel comes after the father and attacks him.
Ⓒ The boy's prediction is accurate. There is no difference.
Ⓓ The father is not happy with the boy's instructions.

"The Smith and the Fairies": A Gaelic Folk Tale (Ed. Kate Douglas Wiggin)

Years ago there lived in Crossbrig a smith of the name of MacEachern. This man had an only child, a boy of about thirteen or fourteen years of age, cheerful, strong, and healthy. All of a sudden he fell ill; took to his bed and moped whole days away. No one could tell what was the matter with him, and the boy himself could not, or would not, tell how he felt. He was wasting away fast; getting thin, old, and yellow; and his father and all his friends were afraid that he would die.

At last one day, after the boy had been lying in this condition for a long time, getting neither better nor worse, always confined to bed, but with an extraordinary appetite—one day, while sadly revolving these things, and standing idly at his forge, with no heart to work, the smith was agreeably surprised to see an old man, well known for his sagacity and knowledge of out-of-the-way things, walk into his workshop. Forthwith he told him the occurrence which had clouded his life.

The old man looked grave as he listened; and after sitting a long time pondering over all he had heard, gave his opinion thus: "It is not your son you have got. The boy has been carried away by the 'Daione Sith,' and they have left a Sibhreach in his place."

"Alas! and what then am I to do?" said the smith. "How am I ever to see my own son again?"
"I will tell you how," answered the old man. "But, first, to make sure that it is not your own son you have got, take as many empty egg-shells as you can get, go into his room, spread them out carefully before his sight, then proceed to draw water with them, carrying them two and two in your hands as if they were a great weight, and arrange them when full, with every sort of earnestness around the fire." The smith accordingly gathered as many broken egg-shells as he could get, went into the room, and proceeded to carry out all his instructions.

He had not been long at work before there arose from the bed a shout of laughter, and the voice of the seeming sick boy exclaimed, "I am eight hundred years of age, and I have never seen the like of that before." The smith returned and told the old man.

"Well, now," said the sage to him, "did I not tell you that it was not your son you had: your son is in Borracheill in a digh there (that is, a round green hill frequented by fairies). Get rid as soon as possible of this intruder, and I think I may promise you your son. You must light a very large and bright fire before the bed on which this stranger is lying. He will ask you, 'What is the use of such a fire as that?' Answer him at once, 'You will see that presently!' and then seize him, and throw him into the middle of it. If it is your own son you have got, he will call out to you to save him; but if not, the thing will fly through the roof."

The smith again followed the old man's advice: kindled a large fire, answered the question put to him as he had been directed to do, and seizing the child flung him in without hesitation. The Sibhreach gave an awful yell, and sprang through the roof, where a hole had been left to let the smoke out.

On a certain night the old man told him the green round hill, where the fairies kept the boy, would be open, and on that date the smith, having provided himself with a Bible, a dirk, and a crowing cock, was to proceed to the hill. He would hear singing and dancing, and much merriment going on, he had been told, but he was to advance boldly; the Bible he carried would be a certain safeguard to him against any danger from the fairies. On entering the hill he was to stick the dirk in the threshold, to prevent the hill from closing upon him; "and then," continued the old man, "on entering you will see a spacious apartment before you, beautifully clean, and there, standing far within, working at a forge, you will also see your own son. When you are questioned, say you come to seek him, and will not go without him."

Not long after this, the time came round, and the smith sallied forth, prepared as instructed. Sure enough as he approached the hill, there was a light where light was seldom seen before. Soon after, a sound of piping, dancing, and joyous merriment reached the anxious father on the night wind.

Overcoming every impulse to fear, the smith approached the threshold steadily, stuck the dirk into it as directed, and entered. Protected by the Bible he carried on his breast, the fairies could not touch him; but they asked him, with a good deal of displeasure, what he wanted there. He answered, "I want my son, whom I see down there, and I will not go without him."

Upon hearing this the whole company before him gave a loud laugh, which wakened up the cock he carried dozing in his arms, who at once leaped up on his shoulders, clapped his wings lustily, and crowed loud and long.

The fairies, incensed, seized the smith and his son, and throwing them out of the hill, flung the dirk after them, and in an instant all was dark.

For a year and a day the boy never did a turn of work, and hardly ever spoke a word; but at last one day, sitting by his father and watching him finishing a sword he was making for some chief, and which he was very particular about, he suddenly exclaimed, "That is not the way to do it;" and taking the tools from his father's hands he set to work himself in his place, and soon fashioned a sword, the like of which was never seen in the country before.

From that day the young man wrought constantly with his father, and became the inventor of a peculiarly fine and well-tempered weapon, the making of which kept the two smiths, father and son, in constant employment, spread their fame far and wide, and gave them the means in abundance, as they before had the disposition, to live content with all the world and very happily with each other.

5. How is the fairy pretend version of the smith's son different than the smith's actual son?

Ⓐ The fairy is a humorous trickster, while the real son is quiet and serious.
Ⓑ The fairy is cruel to the father, while the real son is kind to his father.
Ⓒ The fairy and the son are exactly alike.
Ⓓ The fairy and the father are alike.

Day 12

Rational Numbers As Quotients of Integers (7.NS.A.2.B)

1. Which of the following division problems CANNOT be completed?

    Ⓐ $10 \div 0$
    Ⓑ $155 \div (-3)$
    Ⓒ $(2/3) \div (1/4)$
    Ⓓ $0 \div 5$

2. Which of the following is NOT equivalent to the given value?:

    $\dfrac{3}{4}$

    Ⓐ $\dfrac{-2}{(3)}$

    Ⓑ $\dfrac{-2}{(-3)}$

    Ⓒ $\dfrac{2}{(-3)}$

    Ⓓ All are equivalent values

3. Jared hiked a trail that is 12 miles long. He hiked the trail in section that were 1.5 miles each. In how many sections did he complete the hike?

    Ⓐ 12
    Ⓑ 10
    Ⓒ 8
    Ⓓ 6

"Paul Revere's Ride" (Excerpt)
Henry Wadsworth Longfellow

Listen my children and you shall hear
Of the midnight ride of Paul Revere,
On the eighteenth of April, in Seventy-five;
Hardly a man is now alive
Who remembers that famous day and year.
He said to his friend, "If the British march
By land or sea from the town to-night,
Hang a lantern aloft in the belfry arch
Of the North Church tower as a signal light,--
One if by land, and two if by sea;
And I on the opposite shore will be,
Ready to ride and spread the alarm
Through every Middlesex village and farm,
For the country folk to be up and to arm."
Then he said "Good-night!" and with muffled oar
Silently rowed to the Charlestown shore,
Just as the moon rose over the bay,
Where swinging wide at her moorings lay
The Somerset, British man-of-war;
A phantom ship, with each mast and spar
Across the moon like a prison bar,
And a huge black hulk, that was magnified
By its own reflection in the tide.

It was twelve by the village clock
When he crossed the bridge into Medford town.
He heard the crowing of the cock,
And the barking of the farmer's dog,
And felt the damp of the river fog,
That rises after the sun goes down.
It was one by the village clock,
When he galloped into Lexington.
He saw the gilded weathercock

Swim in the moonlight as he passed,
And the meeting-house windows, black and bare,
Gaze at him with a spectral glare,
As if they already stood aghast
At the bloody work they would look upon.
It was two by the village clock,
When he came to the bridge in Concord town.
He heard the bleating of the flock,

And the twitter of birds among the trees,
And felt the breath of the morning breeze
Blowing over the meadow brown.
And one was safe and asleep in his bed
Who at the bridge would be first to fall,
Who that day would be lying dead,
Pierced by a British musket ball.
You know the rest. In the books you have read
How the British Regulars fired and fled,---
How the farmers gave them ball for ball,
From behind each fence and farmyard wall,
Chasing the redcoats down the lane,
Then crossing the fields to emerge again
Under the trees at the turn of the road,
And only pausing to fire and load.

The Real Story of Revere's Ride
From the Paul Revere House official Website
In 1774 and the Spring of 1775 Paul Revere was employed by the Boston Committee of Correspondence and the Massachusetts Committee of Safety as an express rider to carry news, messages, and copies of resolutions as far away as New York and Philadelphia.

On the evening of April 18, 1775, Paul Revere was sent for by Dr. Joseph Warren and instructed to ride to Lexington, Massachusetts, to warn Samuel Adams and John Hancock that British troops were marching to arrest them. After being rowed across the Charles River to Charlestown by two associates, Paul Revere borrowed a horse from his friend Deacon John Larkin. While in Charlestown, he verified that the local "Sons of Liberty" committee had seen his pre-arranged signals. (Two lanterns had been hung briefly in the bell-tower of Christ Church in Boston, indicating that troops would row "by sea" across the Charles River to Cambridge, rather than marching "by land" out Boston Neck. Revere had arranged for these signals the previous weekend, as he was afraid that he might be prevented from leaving Boston).

On the way to Lexington, Revere "alarmed" the country-side, stopping at each house, and arrived in Lexington about midnight. As he approached the house where Adams and Hancock were staying, a sentry asked that he not make so much noise. "Noise!" cried Revere, "You'll have noise enough before long. The regulars are coming out!" After delivering his message, Revere was joined by a second rider, William Dawes, who had been sent on the same errand by a different route. Deciding on their own to continue on to Concord, Massachusetts, where weapons and supplies were hidden, Revere and Dawes were joined by a third rider, Dr. Samuel Prescott. Soon after, all three were arrested by a British patrol. Prescott escaped almost immediately, and Dawes soon after. Revere was held for some time and then released. Left without a horse, Revere returned to Lexington in time to witness part of the battle on the Lexington Green.

4. According to the poem, what was the purpose of Revere's ride?

- Ⓐ   To alert everyone in the county that the British were approaching.
- Ⓑ   To warn Samuel Adams and John Hancock that the British were approaching.
- Ⓒ   To make it back to Boston in time for the battle.
- Ⓓ   To reach Lexington before the British troops to awaken the members of the militia.

5. According to the non-fiction passage, what was the purpose of Revere's ride?

- Ⓐ   To alert everyone in the county that the British were approaching.
- Ⓑ   To warn Samuel Adams and John Hancock that the British were approaching.
- Ⓒ   To make it back to Boston in time for the battle.
- Ⓓ   To reach Lexington before the British troops to awaken the members of the militia.

Strategies for Multiplying and Dividing Rational Numbers (7.NS.A.2.C)

Day 13

1. Find the product: $3x \dfrac{1}{3}$

   (A) 1
   (B) 3
   (C) 9
   (D) 6

2. Which property is illustrated in the following statement?

   $(5)(4)(7) = (7)(5)(4)$

   (A) Triple multiplication property
   (B) Distributive property
   (C) Commutative property of multiplication
   (D) Associative property of multiplication

3. Find the quotient: $4 \div \dfrac{1}{2}$

   (A) 4
   (B) 8
   (C) 2
   (D) 16

Key Ideas and Details (RI.7.1)

Day 13

From <u>Guiseppi Verdi</u> by Thomas Trapper

Whenever the organ man came into the village of Roncole, in Italy (where Verdi was born, October 10, 1813), Verdi could not be kept indoors. But he followed the wonderful organ and the wonderful man who played it, all day long, as happy as he could be.

When Giuseppe was seven years old his father, though only a poor innkeeper, bought him a spinet, a sort of small piano. So faithfully did the little boy practice that the spinet was soon quite worn out and new jacks, or hammers, had to be made for it. This was done by Stephen Cavaletti, who wrote a message on one of the jacks telling that he made them anew and covered them with leather, and fixed the pedal, doing all for nothing, because the little boy, Giuseppe Verdi, showed such willingness to practice and to learn. Thus the good Stephen thought this was pay enough.

4. Which sentence from the passage best explains how Verdi felt about his first spinet?

Ⓐ "But he followed the wonderful organ and wonderful man who played it all day long, as happy as he could be."

Ⓑ "So faithfully did the little boy practice that the spinet was soon quite worn out and new jacks, or hammers, had to be made for it."

Ⓒ "...because the little boy, Giuseppe Verdi, showed such willingness to practice and to learn."

Ⓓ "Thus the good Stephen thought this was pay enough."

Skunk Chow

Skunks are <u>omnivores</u>. They can be found eating nuts, berries, roots, leaves, grasses and even some types of fungi (mushroom-like plants). For animals, they enjoy dining on rodents such as mice and rats, insects, earthworms, frogs, lizards, toads and birds. Sometimes when they are unable to find live animals to eat they become scavengers eating dead animals left behind. When they live close to people's homes, skunks sometimes will even get into trash cans, eating garbage.

When skunks eat they do not limit themselves to small meals. They like to "pig out" on whatever food they can find. When there is a large amount of food available skunks get very fat very quickly. http://en.wikipedia.org/wiki/Skunk

5. If you had to answer the question "Can skunks control their appetites?" which sentence would you use to support your answer?

Ⓐ "They can be found eating nuts, berries, roots, leaves, grasses, and even some types of fungi (mushroom-like plants)."

Ⓑ "For animals, they enjoy dining on rodents such as mice and rats, insects, earth worms, frogs, lizards, toads, and birds."

Ⓒ "When they live close to people's homes, skunks sometimes will even get into trash cans, eating garbage."

Ⓓ "They like to 'pig out' on whatever food they can find. When there is a large amount of food, skunks get fat very quickly."

Converting Between Rational Numbers and Decimals (7.NS.A.2.D)

Day 14

1. Convert to a decimal: $\dfrac{7}{8}$

   Ⓐ 0.78
   Ⓑ 0.81
   Ⓒ 0.875
   Ⓓ 0.925

2. Convert to a decimal: $\dfrac{5}{6}$

   Ⓐ 0.8333333...
   Ⓑ 0.56
   Ⓒ 0.94
   Ⓓ 0.8

3. How can you tell that the following number is a rational number?

   0.251

   Ⓐ It is a rational number because the decimal terminates.
   Ⓑ It is a rational number because there is a value of 0 in the ones place.
   Ⓒ It is a rational number because the sum of the digits is less than 10.
   Ⓓ It is a rational number because it is not a repeating decimal.

Day 14

Get Right to the Point (RI.7.2)

Fall Leaves
USDA Forest Service

We almost always think of trees as being green, but there is one time of year when their leaves turn a myriad orange, red, yellow and brown: the beautiful and chilly days of fall. Those living in the Eastern or Northern United States come to anticipate the change in color starting in September or October every single year. But what causes the leaves to change color, and why?

Just like many animals that hibernate for the winter, trees experience a unique change during the winter months. During summer, for instance, plants use the process of photosynthesis to transform carbon dioxide found in the air into organic compounds like sugars using energy from the sun. During the winter, however, there is less light to go around, and their ability to create food from the photosynthesis process is limited.

What does that have to do with a leaf's color? The substance that allows trees to turn carbon dioxide into food (chlorophyll) is also the cause for the leaf's green sheen. As the photosynthesis process wanes in the colder months due to the lack of sun, so does its greenish hue, allowing other elements present in the leaf to show through. Believe it or not, the yellows and oranges that appear in fall have actually been there all year in the form of nutrients like carotene (also found in carrots). The intense green color of the chlorophyll had simply overshadowed them. But what about the reds and browns? And what causes the leaves to fall away after they change color?

The bright reds and purples in each leaf come from a strong antioxidant that many trees create on their own because of their protective qualities. The antioxidant helps protect the trees from the sun, lower their freezing levels, and protect them from frost. As winter comes, so does the need for the antioxidant (similar to the way a dog gets more fur during winter to stay warmer).

As for the leaves falling, that is another story. At the base of each leaf, there is a layer of cells that carry food and water from the leaf to the tree during the summer months to keep it fed. In the fall, that layer actually starts to harden, preventing the passage of nutrients. Because of this, the nutrients and waste that previously passed from the leaf into the tree become trapped in the leaf with no fresh water to clean it. Not only does this cause the leaf to turn brown, eventually it causes the cells within it to harden so much that the leaf tears and blows away. Thus the pile of leaves you enjoyed jumping in as a child.

Because each tree, and each leaf, contains a unique amount of nutrients depending on how well-nourished it was over the spring and summer, the way each leaf breaks down during the winter months is also quite different. The result is the unique and complex facet of colors we see in each neighborhood or forest each fall.

http://www.sciencemadesimple.com/leaves.htm

4. What is the main theme of the above passage?

Ⓐ **Fall weather**
Ⓑ **What happens to the leaves during fall**
Ⓒ **The life cycle of a tree during fall**
Ⓓ **Weather during fall**

History of Olympics
From *Ancient Olympics Guide*

Even though the modern Olympic Games are held every four years, they bear little resemblance to the athletic contests held at Olympia in Greece in ancient times.

The games were open to competitors from all Greece, and the contests included chariot racing, horse racing, running, wrestling, boxing, and the pentathlon, a contest involving jumping, quoit-throwing, javelin throwing, running and wrestling.

Scholars date the earliest contests at 776 B.C., more than two and a half thousand years ago. The first trophies that were won consisted not of gold medals and cups but of simple crowns of olive leaves. Women and slaves were admitted neither as contestants nor as spectators. The classical games ceased to be held probably about A.D.393.

Much of the credit for the revival of the Games held at Athens in 1896 goes to Baron Pierre de Coubertin, a French classical scholar, who greatly admired the sporting ideals of the ancient Greeks. As an educationist and lover of amateurism, he looked upon physical exercise as an essential feature of balanced education. Forty-two events were contested and new disciplines such as cycling, hurdling, the high jump, shooting and gymnastics were introduced.

One of the most popular events of the modern Olympics is the marathon. This very tiring twenty-six mile foot race over an open course is the supreme test of the runners' endurance. The marathon was not a part of the ancient Olympics although it originated in Greece.

And, finally, a more recent development in the Olympics is the introduction of the winter games, which were started in 1924. They are held separately from the summer games but in the same year. The Winter Olympics provide competition in skiing, speed and figure skating, ice hockey, and rifle shooting. Such cold weather sports could never have developed in the warm climate of Greece.

5. Choose a suitable alternate title for this passage.

Ⓐ **The Winter Sports**
Ⓑ **The Games' Growth**
Ⓒ **How the Olympics Evolved**
Ⓓ **Popular Sports**

Solving Real World Problems (7.NS.A.3)

Day 15

1. Andrew has $9.39 but needs $15.00 to make a purchase. How much more does he need?

   Ⓐ $6.39
   Ⓑ $5.61
   Ⓒ $5.39
   Ⓓ $6.61

2. Ben has to unload a truck filled with 25 bags of grain for his horses. Each bag weighs 50.75 pounds.

   How many total pounds does he have to move?

   Ⓐ 12,687.50 pounds
   Ⓑ 1,268.75 pounds
   Ⓒ 126.875 pounds
   Ⓓ 1250 pounds

3. A Chinese restaurant purchased 1528.80 pounds of rice. If they received 50 identical bags, how much rice was in each bag?

   Ⓐ 30.576 pounds
   Ⓑ 305.76 pounds
   Ⓒ 3.0576 pounds
   Ⓓ None of the above.

Day 15

Read the following Aesop's Fable and answer the question below.

In a field one summer's day, a Grasshopper was hopping about, chirping and singing to its heart's content. An Ant passed by, bearing along with great toil an ear of corn he was taking to the nest.

"Why not come and chat with me," said the Grasshopper, "instead of toiling and moiling in that way?"
"I am helping to lay up food for the winter," said the Ant, "and recommend you to do the same."
"Why bother about winter?" said the Grasshopper; we have got plenty of food at present." But the Ant went on its way and continued its toil.

When the winter came, the Grasshopper found itself dying of hunger, while it saw the ants distributing, every day, corn and grain from the stores they had collected in the summer.

Then the Grasshopper knew...
It is best to prepare for the days of necessity.

4. What type of relationship do the Grasshopper and the Ant have?

- Ⓐ The Ant and the Grasshopper might be best friends and always help each other.
- Ⓑ The Ant and the Grasshopper might be enemies and never help each other.
- Ⓒ The Ant and the Grasshopper might be acquaintances and have different ways of life.
- Ⓓ The Ant and the Grasshopper are related to each other.

5. What would have happened if the Ant had joined the Grasshopper for a chat?

- Ⓐ The Ant and the Grasshopper would have both starved during the winter.
- Ⓑ The Ant and the Grasshopper would have both had plenty of food for the winter.
- Ⓒ The Ant and the Grasshopper would never have spent any time together.
- Ⓓ The Ant and the Grasshopper would have chatted while they gathered food.

Week 3 Online Activity

Login to the Lumos student account and complete the following activities.

1. Reading assignment
2. Vocabulary practice
3. Write your summer diary

If you haven't created your Lumos account, use the URL and access code below to get started.

URL: http://www.lumoslearning.com/a/tedbooks

Access Code: G7-8MLSLH-19562

Applying Properties to Rational Expressions (7.EE.A.1)

Day 16

1. Ruby is two years younger than her brother. If Ruby's brother's age is A, which of the following expressions correctly represents Ruby's age?

   Ⓐ A - 2
   Ⓑ A + 2
   Ⓒ 2A
   Ⓓ 2 - A

2. Find the difference: $8n - (3n-6) =$

   Ⓐ -n
   Ⓑ 5n - 6
   Ⓒ 5n + 6
   Ⓓ 8n - 6

3. Find the sum:

   $6t + (3t - 5) =$

   Ⓐ 9t - 5
   Ⓑ 9t + 5
   Ⓒ 3t - 5
   Ⓓ 6t - 5

Day 16

From "Bruno the Bear"

The bear became very attached to our two dogs and to all the children living in and around our farm. He was left quite free in his younger days and spent his time in playing, running into the kitchen and going to sleep in our beds.

One day an accident befell him. I put down poison (barium carbonate) to kill the rats and mice that had got into my library. Bruno entered the library as he often did, and ate some of the poison. Paralysis set in to the extent that he could not stand on his feet. But he dragged himself on his stumps to my wife, who called me. I guessed what had happened. Off I rushed him in the car to the vet's residence. A case of poisoning! Tame Bear—barium carbonate—what to do?

Out came his medical books, and a feverish reference to index began: "What poison did you say, sir?" he asked

"Barium carbonate" I said.

"Ah yes—B—Ba—Barium Salts—Ah! Barium carbonate! Symptoms— paralysis—treatment—injections of . .. Just a minute, sir. I'll bring my syringe and the medicine." Said the doc. I dashed back to the car. Bruno was still floundering about on his stumps, but clearly he was weakening rapidly; there was some vomiting, he was breathing heavily, with heaving flanks and gaping mouth. I was really scared and did not know what to do. I was feeling very guilty and was running in and out of the vet's house doing everything the doc asked me.

"Hold him, everybody!" In goes the hypodermic—Bruno squeals — 10 c.c. of the antidote enters his system without a drop being wasted. Ten minutes later: condition unchanged! Another 10 c.c. Injected! Ten minutes later: breathing less torturous— Bruno can move his arms and legs a little although he cannot stand yet. Thirty minutes later: Bruno gets up and has a great feed! He looks at us disdainfully, as much as to say, 'What's barium carbonate to a big black bear like me?' Bruno was still eating. I was really happy to see him recover.

4. Which quality does barium carbonate NOT have?

Ⓐ **It is poisonous to animals.**
Ⓑ **It is used to get rid of rodents.**
Ⓒ **It is safe for animals except rodents.**
Ⓓ **It can cause paralysis.**

From <u>Guiseppi Verdi</u> by Thomas Trapper

Whenever the organ man came into the village of Roncole, in Italy (where Verdi was born, October 10, 1813), Verdi could not be kept indoors. But he followed the wonderful organ and the wonderful man who played it, all day long, as happy as he could be.

When Giuseppe was seven years old his father, though only a poor innkeeper, bought him a spinet, a sort of small piano. So faithfully did the little boy practice that the spinet was soon quite worn out and new jacks, or hammers, had to be made for it. This was done by Stephen Cavaletti, who wrote a message on one of the jacks telling that he made them anew and covered them with leather, and fixed the pedal, doing all for nothing, because the little boy, Giuseppe Verdi, showed such willingness to practice and to learn. Thus the good Stephen thought this was pay enough.

5. **Based on the information in these paragraphs, what musical instrument can you infer the spinet is most like?**

   Ⓐ **A piano**
   Ⓑ **A trumpet**
   Ⓒ **A violin**
   Ⓓ **An electric keyboard**

Day 17

1. Which of the following expressions represents "5% of a number"?

   Ⓐ 5n
   Ⓑ 0.5n
   Ⓒ 0.05n
   Ⓓ 500n

2. Jill is shopping at a department store that is having a sale this week. The store has advertised 15% off certain off-season merchandise. Jill calculates the sales price by multiplying the regular price by 15% and then subtracting that amount from the regular price: SP = RP - 0.15(RP), where S = Sales Price and R = Regular Price. Find a simpler way for Jill to calculate the sales price as she shops.

   Ⓐ SP = 0.15 RP
   Ⓑ SP = 1.15RP
   Ⓒ SP = 0.85RP
   Ⓓ SP = 1.85RP

3. Rewrite the following expression for the perimeter of a rectangle.

   P = l + w + l + w, where P = perimeter, l = length, and w = width.

   Ⓐ P = l + 2w
   Ⓑ P = l + w
   Ⓒ P = 2(l) + w
   Ⓓ P = 2(l + w)

How is it Built? Analyzing Structure (RI.7.5)

Day 17

Bushmen

With so much technology around us each day, it is hard to imagine that anyone in the world would live without television, let alone a cell phone or radio. Still, there are a few cultures that maintain an extremely primitive lifestyle, nearly untouched by the modern world. One of those is commonly known as the Bushmen of Kalahari.

The Bushmen, also known as the "Basarwa" or "San" are found throughout southern Africa in regions of the Kalahari Desert. Nomadic hunters and gatherers by nature, they roam the region living in small kinship groups and, relatively isolated from the rest of society, have developed an extremely unique culture not otherwise seen or understood by modern man.

Unlike English, which is built on a complex system of sounds and letters, the Bushmen speak an extremely unique language made exclusively of clicking sounds. The sounds are created with a sucking action from the tongue, and even the click language itself can vary widely from tribe to tribe, making it extremely difficult to communicate with non-Bush people.

In addition to language, the Bushmen have a very different way of living. Similar to Eskimos, groups of Bushmen will live in "kinship" societies. Led by their elders, they travel together, with women in the group gathering food while men hunt for it. Children, on the other hand, have no duties other than playing. In fact, leisure is an extremely important part of the Bushmen society. Dance, music and humor are essential, with a focus on family rather than technology or development. Because of this, some people associate the Bush culture with a backward kind of living or low status.

Because of the increased speed of advancement and urban development, the Bushmen culture is in danger. Some have already been forced to switch from hunting to farming due to modernization programs in their countries. Others have been forced to move to certain areas of their countries so that modernization can continue to occur there. With so much development, it's clear that though the Bushmen culture is very rich, it is also in danger of extinction. It is unclear how long the Bush culture will continue.

http://en.wikibooks.org/wiki/Cultural_Anthropology/Print_version'

4. How are the paragraphs in this selection organized?

Ⓐ by topic
Ⓑ from broad ideas to narrow ideas
Ⓒ chronologically
Ⓓ compare and contrast

Baseball Card Collecting

Looking for a new hobby? Do you like baseball? If you answered "yes" to these two questions baseball card collecting might be a fun pastime for you to begin! Ever since candy and gum manufacturers started putting cards with pictures of popular baseball players into the packages in the 1800's to encourage young people to buy their sweets, kids have been collecting baseball cards. Now, more than 200 years later, baseball card collecting has become a popular hobby for children and adults alike.

What You Need to Be a Baseball Card Collector

The main thing you need to start a baseball card collection is cards, of course! Baseball cards are usually sold in packs of four or more cards. Large chain stores like Walmart and Target, as well as drug stores, are the easiest places to find packs of baseball cards. You can also find cards at special baseball card shops. You should plan on spending around $2.99 for each pack of baseball cards you purchase. Once you've started your collection by buying packs of cards, you'll probably find that there are one or two specific cards you want that you haven't been able to get in packs. The best places to get single cards are the baseball card shows held at malls or convention centers or on the Internet. You can also trade cards with another baseball card collector. A lot of times, a friend has the card you're looking for. Because you might also have a card he or she wants, trading is a great way to build the collection that you want. Plus, it doesn't cost you a cent!

As a baseball card collector you'll not only need cards, but also a place to put them. Baseball cards can become very valuable. You may get a card in a pack today that is worth ten or twenty times the price you paid for it years down the line. The price that you can sell a baseball card for is based on the condition that it is in. For this reason, you want to be sure to have a safe place to store your cards where they won't get damaged. There are lots of different options for storing baseball cards. If you have just a few important cards that you want to protect you can purchase sleeves to store them in. Sleeves are firm plastic wrappers that are slightly larger than a card. You simply slip the card into the opening on the sleeve and it is protected from wetness and bending. If you have several cards to store, consider buying boxes or albums. At baseball card shops, you can buy boxes that are specially designed to store baseball cards. For serious baseball card collectors with very valuable cards, cases that lock are the ideal spot to store your cards.

Once you've collected cards for a while you'll want a way to keep track of what cards you have in your collection. Those with small collections can use a notebook where they write down the players' names and dates of the cards they have. For those with larger collections, the computer is best place to keep track of their collections. While you can create your own database of cards using a software program on your computer, there are also special baseball card software programs that make it much easier. Beckett, the company that publishes a most popular guide to baseball card values, sells a computer program with the names of cards already loaded into it. You simply need to go in and click on the names of cards to record those that are part of your collection.

Types of Baseball Cards You Can Collect

There are four main companies that produce baseball cards: Topps, Upper Deck, Fleer and Donruss/Playoff. The most popular and easiest cards to find in stores are those made by Topps and Upper Deck. Each of these companies sells sets of cards. You can either purchase a full set from a baseball card store or show or you can put together a set by buying enough packs of cards to collect each card in the set. The basic set put out each year by each company is made up of 500 or more cards. Cards feature posed pictures of Major League Baseball players as well as action shots. Within the basic set, there are several subsets that each has a special theme. For example, a card set might have a special subset of homerun heroes within the larger basic set they sell that year. If you buy individual packs of baseball cards to build your set you'll have a chance at getting insert cards. These are special cards that are printed in limited quantities and are inserted into packs. Insert cards are usually worth more money than basic cards because there are fewer of them produced each year.

For serious baseball collectors there are premium and specialty cards available. Premium cards come in sets and are printed by the main baseball card companies. These cards are more expensive, but feature extra perks. For example, parallel sets of premium cards are the same as the basic set, but are fancier. They might have bolder colors or special borders. In addition to premium sets, serious baseball card collectors like to collect rookie cards. A rookie card is a player's first baseball card. The year that the player is placed on a team's roster he becomes a rookie. Rookie cards become very valuable when the player goes on to have a successful career. Autographed baseball cards are another great find for devoted baseball card collectors. There are two types of autographed cards: those with autographs signed on the actual card and those with autographs cut from other sources that are glued onto the card. This second type are known as cut autos. Cut autos are usually created for players who are no longer living.

A new type of baseball cards has just come out in the last few years and may totally change card collecting in the future. Digital baseball cards are now available. These cards don't come printed on paper like traditional baseball cards. Instead, they are purchased and stored on the Internet. One of the major companies, Topps, has already had great success with their line of computer-based cards called eTopps.

Whatever type of cards you choose to collect, you're sure to find hours of enjoyment in with your new hobby.

http://en.wikibooks.org/wiki/Cultural_Anthropology/Print_version'

5. **If you wanted to find information about how to start a baseball card collection, which section of this selection would you want to read?**

   Ⓐ **what you need to be a baseball card collector**
   Ⓑ **types of baseball cards you can collect**
   Ⓒ **what companies make baseball cards**
   Ⓓ **looking for a new hobby**

Modeling Using Equations or Inequalities (7.EE.B.3)

Day 18

1. A 30 gallon overhead tank was slowly filled with water through a tap. The amount of water (W, in gallons) that is filled over a period of t hours can be found using W = 3.75(t). If the tap is opened at 7 AM and closed at 3 PM, how much water would be in the tank? Assume that the tank is empty before opening the tap.

   Ⓐ 18 gallons
   Ⓑ 20 gallons
   Ⓒ 24 gallons
   Ⓓ The tank is full

2. The ratio (by volume) of milk to water in a certain solution is 3 to 8. If the total volume of the solution is 187 cubic feet, what is the volume of water in the solution?

   Ⓐ 130 cubic feet
   Ⓑ 132 cubic feet
   Ⓒ 134 cubic feet
   Ⓓ 136 cubic feet

3. A box has a length of 12 inches and width of 10 inches. If the volume of the box is 960 cubic inches, what is its height?

   Ⓐ 6 inches
   Ⓑ 10 inches
   Ⓒ 12 inches
   Ⓓ 8 inches

Day 18

From <u>Guiseppi Verdi</u> by Thomas Trapper

Whenever the organ man came into the village of Roncole, in Italy (where Verdi was born, October 10, 1813), Verdi could not be kept indoors. But he followed the wonderful organ and the wonderful man who played it, all day long, as happy as he could be.

When Giuseppe was seven years old his father, though only a poor innkeeper, bought him a spinet, a sort of small piano. So faithfully did the little boy practice that the spinet was soon quite worn out and new jacks, or hammers, had to be made for it. This was done by Stephen Cavaletti, who wrote a message on one of the jacks telling that he made them anew and covered them with leather, and fixed the pedal, doing all for nothing, because the little boy, Giuseppe Verdi, showed such willingness to practice and to learn. Thus the good Stephen thought this was pay enough.

4. Based on these paragraphs, what can you infer the author's view of Verdi is?

- Ⓐ He is amazed by Verdi's talent.
- Ⓑ He thinks Verdi started playing an instrument at too young of an age.
- Ⓒ He is jealous of Verdi's talent.
- Ⓓ He is unsure what to make of Verdi's talent.

<u>The Great Round World and What's Going On In It</u> magazine article

The Czar of Russia is quite ill, and everyone feels sorry that he should be sick now when his advice and assistance are so badly needed to settle the worrying Turkish question, which has so troubled Europe.

The young Czar Nicholas, who was crowned with so much pomp and glory at Moscow last August, seems unable to carry on the government of Russia.

Many people say he is too weak to govern, and that there are going to be troubles and revolts in Russia.

The truth of the matter seems to be, that the young Czar is a gentle, kind-hearted man, who will not govern Russia in the stern, cruel way that his forefathers have done, and who is therefore thought to be weak and incapable.

While he is making a part of his people love him for his goodness, by far the larger half, who have, under the old rule, been able to make money and gain great power, are furious against him.

Poor young Nicholas is not only hated by the people who were most friendly to his father, but by the Nihilists, who look upon him as their natural enemy, and, between the two parties, it is said that the Czar goes about in constant fear of his life.

Nicholas never wanted to be a ruler. Those who know him say that he has become grave and sad in the few months since he came to the throne.

It is said that he is of too gentle a disposition to be able to keep his ministers in order and that they quarrel fiercely in his presence, and show very little respect for him.

According to all accounts, his health is giving way under the constant worry, and it is reported that he received a shock a few weeks ago, which so completely upset him, that it brought on his present illness.

He was walking in his gardens, and wishing to speak to one of the men who was at work; he signaled to him to come to him. The gardener, proud of his sovereign's notice, ran towards him at full speed. But a sentry, who had not noticed the Czar's signal, fearing that the man was going to harm the Emperor, fired his gun at him, and he fell dead at the Czar's feet.

Nicholas was terribly overcome by the dreadful mistake.

Some people say that his present illness is due to anxiety about the Czarina, who is also ill, and again others say that the wound which Nicholas received when he was traveling in Japan is the cause.

He was struck by a crazy Japanese, and would have been killed, had not Prince George of Greece, the son of the present King of Greece, who was with him, warded off the blow. As it was, the blow was heavy enough to form a lump on the young man's skull, which has caused him great pain, and which some people declare is troubling him now.

Whatever the cause, the Czar is ill, and in no state to attend to anything but his own affairs. It is a sad pity just at this moment when Europe needs him so badly.

5. What is the author's view of Czar Nicholas?

Ⓐ   The author does not have much respect for Nicholas.
Ⓑ   The author feels sympathy and pity for Nicholas.
Ⓒ   The author thinks that Nicholas has no business being a Czar.
Ⓓ   The author thinks Russia is worse off now that Czar Nicholas is its ruler.

Solving Multi-Step Problems (7.EE.B.4.A).

Day 19

1   Bob, the plumber, charges 1/4 the cost of materials as his labor fee. If his current job has a material cost of $130, how much will Bob charge his client (including his labor fee)?

   Ⓐ $162.50
   Ⓑ $32.50
   © $130.25
   Ⓓ None of the above

2. A box has a length of 6x inches. The width equals one third the length, and the height equals half the length. If the volume equals 972 cubic inches, what does x equal?

   Ⓐ 5
   Ⓑ 2
   © 3
   Ⓓ 4

3. Taylor is trimming the shrubbery along three sides of his backyard. The backyard is rectangular in shape. The length of the backyard is twice its width and the total perimeter is 180 feet.

   The shrubbery that Taylor needs to trim is along three sides of the rectangular backyard (along the two lengths and one width). Find the total length of the shrubbery that he needs to trim.

   Ⓐ 180 ft
   Ⓑ 60 ft
   © 90 ft
   Ⓓ 120 ft

Day 19

Fall Leaves
USDA Forest Service

We almost always think of trees as being green, but there is one time of year when their leaves turn a myriad orange, red, yellow and brown: the beautiful and chilly days of fall. Those living in the Eastern or Northern United States come to anticipate the change in color starting in September or October every single year. But what causes the leaves to change color, and why?

Just like many animals that hibernate for the winter, trees experience a unique change during the winter months. During summer, for instance, plants use the process of photosynthesis to transform carbon dioxide found in the air into organic compounds like sugars using energy from the sun. During the winter, however, there is less light to go around, and their ability to create food from the photosynthesis process is limited.

What does that have to do with a leaf's color? The substance that allows trees to turn carbon dioxide into food (chlorophyll) is also the cause for the leaf's green sheen. As the photosynthesis process wanes in the colder months due to the lack of sun, so does its greenish hue, allowing other elements present in the leaf to show through. Believe it or not, the yellows and oranges that appear in fall have actually been there all year in the form of nutrients like carotene (also found in carrots). The intense green color of the chlorophyll had simply overshadowed them. But what about the reds and browns? And what causes the leaves to fall away after they change color?

The bright reds and purples in each leaf come from a strong antioxidant that many trees create on their own because of their protective qualities. The antioxidant helps protect the trees from the sun, lower their freezing levels, and protect them from frost. As winter comes, so does the need for the antioxidant (similar to the way a dog gets more fur during winter to stay warmer).

As for the leaves falling, that is another story. At the base of each leaf, there is a layer of cells that carry food and water from the leaf to the tree during the summer months to keep it fed. In the fall, that layer actually starts to harden, preventing the passage of nutrients. Because of this, the nutrients and waste that previously passed from the leaf into the tree become trapped in the leaf with no fresh water to clean it. Not only does this cause the leaf to turn brown, eventually it causes the cells within it to harden so much that the leaf tears and blows away. Thus the pile of leaves you enjoyed jumping in as a child.

Because each tree, and each leaf, contains a unique amount of nutrients depending on how well-nourished it was over the spring and summer, the way each leaf breaks down during the winter months is also quite different. The result is the unique and complex facet of colors we see in each neighborhood or forest each fall.

http://www.sciencemadesimple.com/leaves.htm

4. If this passage was turned into a video documentary, what would it include to help you understand how the leaves change color?

   Ⓐ Time-lapse video of the leaves changing color
   Ⓑ Paintings by artists depicting fall leaves
   Ⓒ Pictures of animals that hibernate during the winter
   Ⓓ Subtitles of the text on the screen

5. You've been asked to turn this passage into a slide show presentation. Which graphic would you use to help explain the process of leaves changing color?

   Ⓐ A picture of leaves that have changed color
   Ⓑ A picture of animals hibernating
   Ⓒ A diagram of the process leaves go through when changing color
   Ⓓ A diagram explaining when leaves change color around the world

Day 20

Linear Inequality Word Problems (7.EE.B.4.B)

1. The annual salary for a certain position depends upon the years of experience of the applicant. The base salary is $50,000, and an additional $3,000 is added to that per year of experience, y, in the field. The company does not want to pay more than $70,000 for this position, though. Which of the following inequalities correctly expresses this scenario?

   Ⓐ $53,000y \leq 70,000$
   Ⓑ $3,000y \leq 50,000$
   Ⓒ $50,000 + 3,000y \leq 70,000$
   Ⓓ $3,000 + 50,000y \leq 70,000$

2. Huck has $225 in savings, and he is able to save an additional $45 per week from his work income. He wants to save enough money to have at least $500 in his savings. If w is the number of weeks, express this situation as an inequality.

   Ⓐ $265w \geq 500$
   Ⓑ $225 + 45w \geq 500$
   Ⓒ $225 \leq 45w$
   Ⓓ $225 + 45w \leq 500$

3. Lucy is charging her phone. It has a 20% charge right now and increases by an additional 2% charge every 3 minutes. She doesn't want to take it off the charger until it is at least 75% charged. If m is the number of minutes Lucy keeps her phone for charging, express this situation in an inequality.

   Ⓐ $20 + \dfrac{2}{3} m \leq 75$

   Ⓑ $20m + \dfrac{2}{3} m \leq 75$

   Ⓒ $75 + \dfrac{2}{3} m \geq 20$

   Ⓓ $20 + \dfrac{2}{3} m \geq 75$

What's the Author's Point? (RI.7.8)

Day 20

Fall Leaves
USDA Forest Service

We almost always think of trees as being green, but there is one time of year when their leaves turn a myriad orange, red, yellow and brown: the beautiful and chilly days of fall. Those living in the Eastern or Northern United States come to anticipate the change in color every year starting in September or October. What causes the leaves to change color, and why?

Just like many animals that hibernate for the winter, trees experience a unique change during the winter months. During summer, plants use the process of photosynthesis to transform carbon dioxide found in the air into organic compounds like sugars using energy from the sun. During the winter, however, there is less light to go around, and their ability to create food from the photosynthesis process is limited. What does that have to do with a leaf's color? The substance that allows trees to turn carbon dioxide into food (chlorophyll) is also the cause for the leaf's green sheen. As the photosynthesis process wanes in the colder months due to the lack of sun, so does its greenish hue, allowing other elements present in the leaf to show through. Believe it or not, the yellows and oranges that appear in fall have actually been there all year in the form of nutrients like carotene (also found in carrots). The intense green color of the chlorophyll had simply overshadowed them.

But what about the reds and browns? And what causes the leaves to fall away after they change color? The bright reds and purples in each leaf come from a strong antioxidant that many trees create on their own because of their protective qualities. The antioxidant helps protect the trees from the sun, lower their freezing levels, and protect them from frost. As winter comes, so does the need for the antioxidant (similar to the way a dog gets more fur during winter to stay warm).

As for the leaves falling, that is another story. At the base of each leaf, there is a layer of cells that carry food and water from the leaf to the tree during the summer months to keep it fed. In the fall, that layer actually starts to harden, preventing the passage of nutrients. Because of this, the nutrients and waste that previously passed from the leaf into the tree become trapped in the leaf with no fresh water to clean it. Not only does this cause the leaf to turn brown, eventually it causes the cells within it to harden so much that the leaf tears and blows away. Thus the pile of leaves you enjoyed jumping in as a child.

Because each tree, and each leaf, contains a unique amount of nutrients depending on how well-nourished it was over the spring and summer, the way each leaf breaks down during the winter months is also quite different. The result is the unique and complex facet of colors we see in neighborhoods and forest each fall.

4. For the information in this selection to be considered reliable, it would need to be written by....

(A) a journalist
(B) a student
(C) a scientist
(D) an environmental activist

Egyptian Pyramids

Today, we have high-tech cranes and other machines to help us create massive skyscrapers and other modern works of architecture. Still, some of the most breath taking architecture in the world, such as the ancient pyramids of Egypt, were created before those high-tech machines even existed. So how did those ancient civilizations create them?

Believe it or not, though they are one of the most studied and admired relics in history, there is no evidence to tell historians exactly how the Ancient Egyptians built the pyramids. Thus, they have been left to create their own theories as to how Egyptians created such amazing and awe-inspiring works of art.

According to one theory, the Egyptians placed logs under the large stone blocks in order to roll or transport them to the pyramid building location. Large groups of men would work to push or pull them into place (although historians also disagree on whether these men were slaves or skilled artisans). Still more, once the men moved the blocks to the pyramid location, they needed to lift them to ever-increasing heights to reach the top levels of the pyramid as it grew. Without modern cranes, many scientists have been baffled as to how they were able to do it. Some believe they used a ramp system that would allow them to roll the blocks upward around or through the pyramids; others believe they must have used a combination of pulleys and lifts. Still, most agree that once they did, they used a mixture of gravel and limestone to help fill any crevices and hold the mound together.

With such a primitive yet impressive building process, it's obvious that the pyramids must have taken a great deal of time to build. With an estimated 2 million blocks weighing an average of 2.5 million tons each, the Great Pyramid of Giza, for instance, is estimated to have taken some 20 years to build. At 481 feet tall, it held the record of tallest building for 3,800 years – not bad for a building created almost entirely by hand.

Even though scientists don't know exactly how the Egyptians did it, they do know that the method the Egyptians used to build pyramids changed over time. In the early days, the pyramids were made completely of stone, with limestone used to create the main body and higher quality limestone being used for the smooth outer casing. Later on, the pyramids were made mostly of mud brick with a limestone casing. Though they were likely much easier to build, they didn't stand up nearly as well over time, leaving archaeologists with even fewer clues about their creation.

5. How could you verify whether or not the information in this selection is accurate?

- Ⓐ **by interviewing the author of the essay**
- Ⓑ **by reading an encyclopedia entry on the Egyptian pyramids**
- Ⓒ **by talking with an Egyptian historian**
- Ⓓ **by going to Egypt**

Week 4 Online Activity

Login to the Lumos student account and complete the following activities.

1. **Reading assignment**
2. **Vocabulary practice**
3. **Write your summer diary**

If you haven't created your Lumos account, use the URL and access code below to get started.

URL: http://www.lumoslearning.com/a/tedbooks

Access Code: G7-8MLSLH-19562

Day 21

1. Triangle ABC and triangle PQR are similar. Find the value of x.

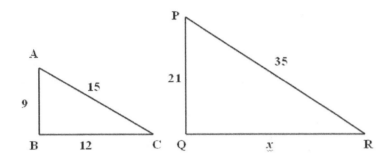

Ⓐ 23
Ⓑ 25
Ⓒ 26
Ⓓ 28

2. If the sides of two similar figures have a similarity ratio of $\dfrac{3}{2}$ what is the ratio of their areas?

Ⓐ $\dfrac{9}{4}$

Ⓑ $\dfrac{3}{2}$

Ⓒ $\dfrac{1}{3}$

Ⓓ $\dfrac{3}{1}$

3. What is the similarity ratio between the following two similar figures?

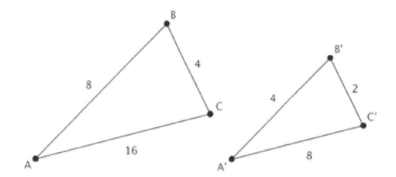

(A) $\dfrac{2}{1}$

(B) $\dfrac{1}{4}$

(C) $\dfrac{2}{3}$

(D) $\dfrac{3}{3}$

Day 21

Equal? Alike? Different? Comparing Authors (RI.7.9)

PASSAGE A:

When I was in the fourth grade, no one liked me because my brother was arrested and that made everyone think that I might do something illegal too. It hurt my feelings to have to sit through school every day and not talk to anyone. When it was time to work in groups, I would have to sit with a group of kids that I knew hated me. Sometimes they would say something mean or move a chair away when it looked like I might sit with them. It was worse during lunch and on the bus when kids would yell things about my brother and ask me if I visited him in prison. After awhile, I didn't want to go to school anymore, and I pretended to be sick every day, so I could stay home. Telling my parents and my teachers didn't change anything. After a while, my parents decided to let me change schools. The first year at my new school was bad because I didn't know anyone and was afraid to talk to people because of everything that happened at the old school. After a while, I made a few friends, and I started to feel better about talking to people. Now I have a few friends, and I don't feel like people are bullying me anymore.

PASSAGE B:

According to Dr. Norman Anderson, CEO of the American Psychological Association, bullying is any kind of aggressive behavior in which someone intentionally tries to harm or cause discomfort to another person. Bullying can be in the form of physical contact but is just as frequently demonstrated in cruel remarks, intentional exclusion of the victim, or in recent years, cyber bullying, in which the aggressor lashes out to the victim via e-mail, social networking, or text messaging.

There is no single, identifiable cause of bullying. Bullying often occurs as a result of influences from peer groups, family groups, community, or even the media. It is, therefore, important to engage all of these groups if any anti-bullying effort is to be successful.

For many years, the primary means employed by schools to deal with student to student bullying has been to punish the aggressor. Research has shown that disciplinary consequences alone will not significantly curb bullying in academic settings. Faculty and administrators must be trained to identify early warning signs that students are either bullies or being bullied, and onlookers, students who are not bullies themselves, but do nothing to inhibit bullying they witness, must be empowered with interpersonal skills training to help them intervene when they witness bullying within their peer groups.

4. According the author of Passage B, what strategy would most likely have helped the author of Passage A?

Ⓐ Disciplinary consequences for the bullies
Ⓑ Changing schools
Ⓒ Training "onlookers" to intervene when they witness bullying
Ⓓ Counseling for the bullying victim

2. What information from Passage B best explains this line from Passage A:

Telling my parents and my teachers didn't change anything.

Ⓐ Faculty and administrators must be trained to identify early warning signs that students are either bullies or being bullied.
Ⓑ Bullying often occurs as a result of influences from peer groups, family groups, community, or even the media.
Ⓒ Bullying can be in the form of physical contact, but is just as frequently demonstrated in cruel remarks, intentional exclusion of the victim, or in recent years, cyber bullying, in which the aggressor lashes out to the victim via e-mail, social networking, or text messaging.
Ⓓ For many years, the primary means employed by schools to deal with student to student bullying has been to punish the aggressor.

Day 22

1. Which of the following lengths cannot be the lengths of the sides of a triangle?

   Ⓐ 4, 6, 9
   Ⓑ 3, 4, 2
   Ⓒ 2, 2, 3
   Ⓓ 1, 1, 2

2. Which of the following set of lengths cannot be the lengths of the sides of a triangle?

   Ⓐ 12.5, 20, 30
   Ⓑ 10, 10, 12
   Ⓒ 4, 8.5, 14
   Ⓓ 3, 3, 3

3. If the measure of two angles in a triangle are 60 and 100 degrees, what is the measure of the third angle?

   Ⓐ 20 degrees
   Ⓑ 50 degrees
   Ⓒ 30 degrees
   Ⓓ 180 degrees

Phrases and Clauses are Coming to Town (L.7.1.A)

Day 22

4. What type of word group is the following?

   Walking down the street

   Ⓐ Phrase
   Ⓑ Dependent Clause
   Ⓒ Independent Clause
   Ⓓ Dependent Phrase

5. What type of word group is the underlined portion of the following sentence?

   After leaving school, <u>I realized I left my science textbook in my locker.</u>

   Ⓐ Phrase
   Ⓑ Dependent Clause
   Ⓒ Independent Clause
   Ⓓ Complete Phrase

Day 23

1. The horizontal cross section of a cylinder is a _____.

   Ⓐ rectangle
   Ⓑ triangle
   Ⓒ circle
   Ⓓ parallelogram

2. In order for a three-dimensional shape to be classified as a "prism," its horizontal cross-sections must be _____.

   Ⓐ congruent polygons
   Ⓑ non-congruent polygons
   Ⓒ circles
   Ⓓ equilateral triangles

3. Which of the following nets is not the net of a cube?

   Ⓐ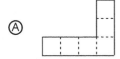

   Ⓑ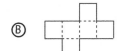

   Ⓒ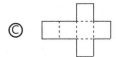

   Ⓓ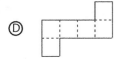

Good Sentences are Built on Agreement (L.7.1.B)

Day 23

4. Which of the following verb forms correctly fills in the blank in the following sentence?

   Almost everybody _____ glad we do not have school next Monday.

   Ⓐ is
   Ⓑ are
   Ⓒ were
   Ⓓ am

5. Which of the following sentences has correct subject-verb agreement?

   Ⓐ Each of my sisters have their rooms.
   Ⓑ Marco's car needs a new transmission and a new clutch.
   Ⓒ My cat don't fit through the kitty door because its stomach is so fat.
   Ⓓ Drinking water help you lose weight.

Day 24

1. A circle is divided into 4 equal sections. What is the measure of each of the angles formed at the center of the circle?

   Ⓐ 25 degree
   Ⓑ 180 degree
   Ⓒ 90 degree
   Ⓓ 360 degree

2. What is the area of a circle with diameter 8 cm? Round your answer to the nearest tenth. Use $\pi = 3.14$.

   Ⓐ 201.1 cm²
   Ⓑ 201.0 cm²
   Ⓒ 50.2 cm²
   Ⓓ 25.1 cm²

3. What is the radius of a circle with a circumference of 125 cm? Round your answer to the nearest whole number. Use $\pi = 3.14$.

   Ⓐ 24 cm
   Ⓑ 10 cm
   Ⓒ 20 cm
   Ⓓ 19 cm

Managing Modifiers (L.7.1.C)

Day 24

4. Which of the following adverbs fits best in the blank in this sentence?

My uncle's computer which was made in 1987 connects _____ to the Internet.

- Ⓐ angrily
- Ⓑ slowly
- Ⓒ quickly
- Ⓓ fast

2. What piece of punctuation should always appear between two coordinate adjectives?

- Ⓐ A semi-colon
- Ⓑ A comma
- Ⓒ A period
- Ⓓ A colon

Day 25

1. Find x.

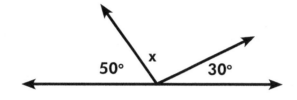

- Ⓐ 40°
- Ⓑ 60°
- Ⓒ 80°
- Ⓓ 100°

2. Find the measures of the missing angles in the figure below.

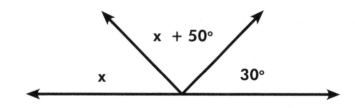

- Ⓐ 30° and 60°
- Ⓑ 60° and 90°
- Ⓒ 50° and 100°
- Ⓓ 60° and 120°

3. The sum of the measures of angles a and b is 155 degrees. What is the measure of angle b?

- Ⓐ 155 degrees
- Ⓑ 77.5 degrees
- Ⓒ 35 degrees
- Ⓓ 210.5 degrees

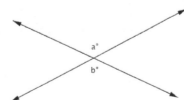

Using Coordinate Adjectives (L.7.2.a)

Day 25

4. Where should a comma be placed in the following sentence?

The fascinating intelligent old man told us all about his experiences during the war.

- (A) fascinating, intelligent
- (B) intelligent, old
- (C) experiences, during
- (D) the, fascinating

5. Which choice best combines the following sentences with coordinate adjectives?

Slippery roads are common during the winter.
Slippery roads are also dangerous roads.

- (A) Slippery and dangerous roads are common during the winter.
- (B) Slippery, dangerous roads are common during the winter.
- (C) Slippery, and also dangerous, roads are common during the winter.
- (D) Slippery roads are common during the winter and are dangerous.

Week 5 Online Activity

Login to the Lumos student account and complete the following activities.

1. Reading assignment
2. Vocabulary practice
3. Write your summer diary

If you haven't created your Lumos account, use the URL and access code below to get started.
URL: http://www.lumoslearning.com/a/tedbooks
Access Code: G7-8MLSLH-19562

Day 26

1. Find the area of the rectangle shown below.

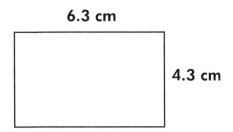

6.3 cm

4.3 cm

Ⓐ 10.5 square centimeters
Ⓑ 24 square centimeters
Ⓒ 27.09 square centimeters
Ⓓ 21 square centimeters

2. What is the volume of a cube whose sides measure 8 inches?

Ⓐ 24 in³
Ⓑ 64 in³
Ⓒ 128 in³
Ⓓ 512 in³

3. Calculate the area of the following polygon.

Ⓐ 15 square units
Ⓑ 30 square units
Ⓒ 36 square units
Ⓓ 18 square units

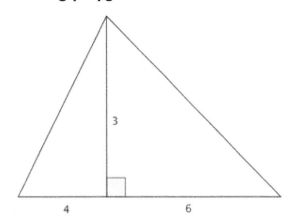

3

4   6

Spellcheck! (L.7.2.B)

Day 26

4. Which word in the following sentence is misspelled?

We all go threw difficult times in our lives when we feel sad and lonely.

Ⓐ threw
Ⓑ difficult
Ⓒ lives
Ⓓ lonely

5. Which of the following word is misspelled?

Ⓐ Fierce
Ⓑ Sleigh
Ⓒ Experement
Ⓓ Weird

Day 27

1. Joe and Mary want to calculate the average height of students in their school. Which of the following groups of students would produce the least amount of bias?

   Ⓐ Every student in the 8th grade.
   Ⓑ Every student on the school basketball team.
   Ⓒ A randomly selected group of students in the halls.
   Ⓓ Joe & Mary's friends.

2. Which of the following represents who you should survey in a population?

   Ⓐ A random, representative group from the population
   Ⓑ Every individual in a population
   Ⓒ Only those in the population that agree with you
   Ⓓ Anyone, including those not in the population

3. What does increasing the sample size of a survey do for the overall results?

   Ⓐ Decreases bias in the results
   Ⓑ Increases the mean of the results
   Ⓒ Increases the reliability of the results
   Ⓓ Increasing sample size does not impact the results of a survey

Precise and Concise Language (L.7.3.A)

Day 27

4. Which choice best rewrites the following sentence with precise, concise language?

I am having a good day.

- Ⓐ I am having a great day.
- Ⓑ I am having a really good day.
- Ⓒ I am having an extremely productive day.
- Ⓓ I am having a really, really good day.

5. Which choice uses the most precise and concise language?

- Ⓐ Hunting animals, like those who are endangered, is very wrong and not okay to do.
- Ⓑ Hunting animals, like those who are endangered, is very wrong.
- Ⓒ Hunting endangered animals is very wrong.
- Ⓓ Hunting endangered animals is illegal.

Day 28

1. John comes up with the following methods for generating unbiased samples from shoppers at a mall.

   I. Ask random strangers in the mall

   II. Always go to the mall at the same time of day

   III. Go to different places in the mall

   IV. Don't ask questions the same way to different people

   Which of these techniques represents the best way of generating an unbiased sample?

   Ⓐ I and II
   Ⓑ I and III
   Ⓒ I, II, and III
   Ⓓ All of these

2. These two samples are about students' favorite subjects. What inference can you make concerning the students' favorite subjects?

Student samples	Science	Math	English Language Arts	Total
#1	40	14	30	84
#2	43	17	33	96

   Ⓐ Students prefer Science over the other subjects.
   Ⓑ Students prefer Math over the other subjects.
   Ⓒ Students prefer English language arts over the other subjects.
   Ⓓ Students prefer History over the other subjects.

3. These two samples are about students' favorite types of movies. What inference can you make concerning the students' favorite types of movies?

Student samples	Action	Drama	Comedy	Total
#1	45	19	35	99
#2	48	22	38	108

Ⓐ Students prefer action movies over the other types.
Ⓑ Students prefer drama over the other types.
Ⓒ Students prefer comedy over the other types.
Ⓓ none

Figuring it out with Context Clues (L.7.4.A)

Day 28

Still, there was something that was bothering Sam. The tryouts for the tennis team were on the same day as his mom's birthday, and he knew his family was planning a huge surprise party for her. He didn't want to hurt his mom's feelings by missing the party, but he also didn't want to miss his one shot at being a champion tennis player just because the tryouts were on his mom's birthday. He was in a quandary; he didn't know what to do.

4. What is the meaning of the word "quandary" in the above passage?

Ⓐ a state of elation
Ⓑ a state of certainty
Ⓒ a state of perplexity
Ⓓ a simple state of mind

Hold him, everybody! In goes the hypodermic—Bruno squeals — 10 c.c. of the antidote enters his system without a drop being wasted. Ten minutes later: condition unchanged! Another 10 c.c. Injected! Ten minutes later: breathing less torturous— Bruno can move his arms and legs a little although he cannot stand yet. Thirty minutes later: Bruno gets up and has a great feed! He looks at us disdainfully, as much as to say, 'What's barium carbonate to a big black bear like me?' Bruno was still eating. I was really happy to see him recover.

5. What is the meaning of the word "hypodermic"?

Ⓐ aortic
Ⓑ skin
Ⓒ orally administered drugs
Ⓓ injection

Day 29

1. Consider the following dot-plot for Height versus Weight.

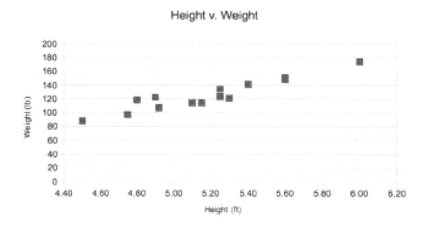

Height v. Weight

What does this dot-plot indicate about the correlation between height and weight?

Ⓐ There is no correlation.
Ⓑ There is a strong negative correlation.
Ⓒ There is a strong positive correlation.
Ⓓ There is a weak positive correlation.

2. The following chart represents the heights of boys on the basketball and soccer teams.

Basketball	Soccer
5′4″	4′11″
5′2″	4′10″
5′3″	5′9″
5′5″	5′1″
5′5″	5′0″
5′1″	5′1″
5′9″	5′3″
5′3″	5′1″

What inference can be made based on this information?

Ⓐ Soccer players have a higher average skill level than basketball players.
Ⓑ Soccer players have a lower average weight than basketball players.
Ⓒ Basketball players have a higher average height than soccer players.
Ⓓ No inference can be made.

3. Use the table below to answer the question that follows:

Month	Avg Temp.
January	24°F
February	36°F
March	55°F
April	65°F
May	72°F
June	78°F

What is difference between the mean temperature of the first four months of the year and the mean temperature of the next two months?

Ⓐ 15 degrees
Ⓑ 20 degrees
Ⓒ 25 degrees
Ⓓ 30 degrees

Re+view – Roots and Affixes (L.7.4.B)

Day 29

4. Determine the meaning of the word autonomous based on the following affixes.

Auto-=self
Nom=order
-ous=having the quality of

Ⓐ ordering something for yourself
Ⓑ being different than other people
Ⓒ having the qualities of self and order
Ⓓ being able to do something by yourself

5. The affix *path* means "to feel". What is the meaning of *empathetic* in the following sentence?

Because Mrs. Anderson is an empathetic person, she tries to help everyone in her church who is suffering.

Ⓐ nice
Ⓑ caring
Ⓒ helpful
Ⓓ cruel

Mean, Median, and Mode (7.SP.B.4)

Day 30

1. The following data set represents a score from 1-10 for a customer's experience at a local restaurant.

    { 1, 1, 2, 1, 3, 4, 7, 8, 1, 3, 4, 2, 1, 3, 7, 2 }

    If a score of 1 means the customer did not have a good experience, and a 10 means the customer had a fantastic experience, what can you infer by looking at the data?

    Ⓐ Overall, customers had a good experience.
    Ⓑ Overall, customers had a bad experience.
    Ⓒ Overall, customers had an "ok" experience.
    Ⓓ Nothing can be inferred from this data.

2. The manager of a local pizza place has asked you to make suggestions on how to improve his menu. The following bar graph represents the results of a survey asking customers what their favorite food at the restaurant was.

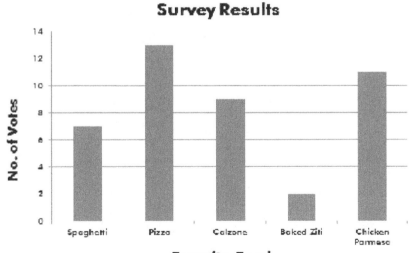

Based on these survey results, which menu item would you suggest the manager remove from the menu?

(A) Spaghetti
(B) Pizza
(C) Calzone
(D) Baked Ziti

3. What are the measures of central tendency?

(A) Mean, Median, Mode
(B) Median, Mode, Mean Absolute Deviation
(C) Median, Mean Absolute Deviation, Sample Size
(D) Mean, Median, Range

4. While reading his science textbook, Jorge comes across the following sentence: Animals are part of different ecosystems around the world.

1. If he wanted to find the meaning of "ecosystems," where would be the best place to look so he can find the definition quickly?

Ⓐ In a dictionary
Ⓑ In the glossary
Ⓒ In a thesaurus
Ⓓ In another chapter

While reading his science textbook, Jorge comes across the following sentence: Animals are part of different ecosystems around the world.

5. If Jorge wanted to find words similar to the word "ecosystems" where would be the best place to look?

Ⓐ In a dictionary
Ⓑ In the glossary
Ⓒ In a thesaurus
Ⓓ In another chapter

Week 6 Online Activity

Login to the Lumos student account and complete the following activities.

1. Reading assignment
2. Vocabulary practice
3. Write your summer diary

If you haven't created your Lumos account, use the URL and access code below to get started.

URL: http://www.lumoslearning.com/a/tedbooks

Access Code: G7-8MLSLH-19562

Day 31

1. Mary has 3 red marbles and 7 yellow marbles in a bag. If she were to remove 2 red and 1 yellow marbles and set them aside, what is the probability of her pulling a yellow marble as her next marble?

   Ⓐ $\dfrac{1}{6}$

   Ⓑ $\dfrac{1}{7}$

   Ⓒ $\dfrac{7}{10}$

   Ⓓ $\dfrac{6}{7}$

2. John has a deck of cards (52 cards). If John removes a number 2 card from the deck, what is the probability that he will pick a number 2 card at random?

   Ⓐ 3 out of 51
   Ⓑ 4 out of 51
   Ⓒ 26 out of 51
   Ⓓ 30 out of 51

3. Maggie has a bag of coins (8 nickels, 6 quarters, 12 dimes, 20 pennies). If she picks a coin at random, what is the probability that she will pick a quarter?

   Ⓐ 2 out of 15
   Ⓑ 3 out of 23
   Ⓒ 3 out of 50
   Ⓓ 5 out of 46

How to Look it Up – Which Fits? Multiple Meaning Words (L.7.4.D)

Day 31

Marta's Language Arts teacher reads the rough draft of an essay Marta wrote for her class. The teacher notices that Marta uses the word great ten times in one paragraph. She suggests Marta find some synonyms for this word to use in place of it.

4. What reference material would help Marta the most?

Ⓐ   a dictionary
Ⓑ   an atlas
Ⓒ   an almanac
Ⓓ   a thesaurus

Nick wants to create a spreadsheet to keep track of the money he has earned by mowing lawns this summer. His uncle buys him a new spreadsheet software program to install on his computer. Nick hasn't used this program before and wants to learn more about it, so he can set up his spreadsheet.

5. What reference material would be most useful for Nick to check out from the library?

Ⓐ   a directory
Ⓑ   a guidebook
Ⓒ   a manual
Ⓓ   a dictionary

Predicting Using Probability (7.SP.C.6)

Day 32

1. Which of the following represents the sample space for flipping two coins?

   Ⓐ {HH, TT}
   Ⓑ {H, T}
   Ⓒ {HH, HT, TH, TT}
   Ⓓ {HH, HT, TT}

2. Which of the following experiments would best test the statement, "The probability of a coin landing on heads is 1/2."?

   Ⓐ Toss a coin 1,000 times, and record the results.
   Ⓑ Toss a coin twice to see if it lands on heads one out of those two times.
   Ⓒ Toss a coin until it lands on heads and record the number of tries it took.
   Ⓓ Toss a coin twice, if it doesn't land on heads exactly once, the theoretical probability is false.

3. Which of the following results is most likely from tossing a six-sided die?

   Ⓐ Rolling an odd number
   Ⓑ Rolling an even number
   Ⓒ Rolling a number from 1 to 3
   Ⓓ All of the above are equally likely.

Give it a Shot – Figures of Speech (L.7.5.A)

Day 32

As soon as Hector ate the fifteenth hotdog, he knew he had made a mistake entering the hot dog eating contest. His stomach felt <u>like a ton of bricks</u> with all that meat and bread in it!

4. What is the meaning of the underlined figure of speech?

Ⓐ light and empty
Ⓑ queasy and nauseous
Ⓒ heavy and full
Ⓓ hard and solid

Kim had spent the last three days writing the speech she was going to give the students during the assembly. She wanted more than anything to be elected as the president of the student council. When she looked down at the paper in her hand, she realized she was holding her math homework, not a copy of the speech. Kim looked up to see hundreds of pairs of eyes looking at her. Not wanting to give up on her dream of being elected and not wanting to appear unprepared, <u>Kim gave her speech off the cuff</u>.

5. What is the meaning of the underlined figure of speech?

Ⓐ quickly
Ⓑ quietly
Ⓒ embarrassedly
Ⓓ freely

Day 33

1. Sara rolls two dice, one black and one yellow. What is the probability that she will roll a 3 on the black die and a 5 on the yellow die?

   Ⓐ $\dfrac{1}{6}$

   Ⓑ $\dfrac{1}{12}$

   Ⓒ $\dfrac{2}{15}$

   Ⓓ $\dfrac{1}{36}$

2. Which of the following represents the probability of an event most likely to occur?

   Ⓐ 0.25
   Ⓑ 0.91
   Ⓒ 0.58
   Ⓓ 0.15

3. Which of the following is not a valid probability?

   Ⓐ 0.25

   Ⓑ $\dfrac{1}{5}$

   Ⓒ 1

   Ⓓ $\dfrac{5}{4}$

We're Related – Word Relationships (L.7.5.B)

4. What is the relationship between the words serial and cereal?

(A) They are synonyms.
(B) They are antonyms.
(C) They are homonyms.
(D) They are opposites.

5. What is the relationship between the words annoying and unpleasant?

(A) They are synonyms.
(B) They are antonyms.
(C) They are homonyms.
(D) They are homographs.

Day 34

Probability Models from Observed Frequencies (7.SP.C.7.B)

1. Felix flipped a coin 8 times and got the following results: H, H, T, H, H, T, T, H. If these results were typical for that coin, what are the odds of flipping a heads with that coin?

   Ⓐ 3 out of 5
   Ⓑ 5 out of 8
   Ⓒ 3 out of 8
   Ⓓ 1 out of 2

2. Bridgette rolled a six-sided die 100 times to test the frequency of each number's appearing. According to these statistics, how many times should a 2 be rolled out of 50 rolls?

Number	Frequency
1	18%
2	20%
3	16%
4	11%
5	18%
6	17%

   Ⓐ 10 times
   Ⓑ 20 times
   Ⓒ 12 times
   Ⓓ 15 times

3. Randomly choosing a number out of a hat 50 times resulted in choosing an odd number a total of four more times than the number of times an even number was chosen. How many times was an even number chosen from the hat?

   Ⓐ 27 times
   Ⓑ 21 times
   Ⓒ 29 times
   Ⓓ 23 times

Would You Rather Own a Boat or a Yacht? Denotation and Connotation (L.7.5.C)

Day 34

Omar is always making jokes and trying to get others to laugh. Even when a situation is serious, he tries to make light of it by joking. When Omar told his friends that his grandmother was very sick and might die, everyone thought he was just joking around. Omar was trying to share something very sad, but his friends thought he was being <u>facetious</u>.

4. The denotation of facetious is "amusing or funny". Based on the context of its use in this paragraph, what is the connotation of the word?

Ⓐ positive
Ⓑ negative

Selma is often late to work, and when she does arrive there, she is lazy and rude to the customers. Selma's boss, Nick, met with her to talk with her about her job performance. Nick said Selma has many good qualities, but he needs to <u>boot</u> her from her job immediately.
The word *boot* means "to end someone's employment".

5. Based on this paragraph, the connotation of this word is...

Ⓐ negative
Ⓑ positive
Ⓒ neutral

Day 35

Find the Probability of a Compound Event (7.SP.C.8.A)

1. The following tree diagram represents Jane's possible outfits:

How many different outfits can Jane make based on this diagram?

Ⓐ 2
Ⓑ 12
Ⓒ 16
Ⓓ 4

2. The following tree diagram represents Jane's possible outfits:

If Jane randomly selects an outfit, what is the probability she will be wearing Jeans AND Sneakers?

Ⓐ $\dfrac{1}{12}$

Ⓑ $\dfrac{1}{3}$

Ⓒ $\dfrac{1}{4}$

Ⓓ $\dfrac{1}{2}$

3. Paul, Jack, Tom, Fred, and Sam are competing in the long jump. If they win the top five spots, how many ways could they be arranged in the top five spots?

Ⓐ 15 ways
Ⓑ 60 ways
Ⓒ 120 ways
Ⓓ 3,125 ways

Grade-Appropriate Vocabulary (L.7.6)

Day 35

"Bruno the Bear"
Excerpt from The Bond of Love

For the next three hours she would not leave that cage. She gave him tea, lemonade, cakes, ice cream and what not. Then 'closing time' came and we had to leave. My wife cried bitterly; Bruno cried bitterly; even the hardened curator and the keepers felt depressed. As for me, I had reconciled myself to what I knew was going to happen next.

"Oh please, sir," she asked the curator, "may I have my Bruno back"?
Hesitantly, he answered, "Madam, he belongs to the zoo and is Government property now. I cannot give away Government property. But if my boss, the superintendent agrees, certainly you may have him back."

There followed the return journey home and a visit to the superintendent's office. A tearful pleading: "Bruno and I are both fretting for each other. Will you please give him back to me?" He was a kind-hearted man and consented. Not only that, but he wrote to the curator telling him to lend us a cage for transporting the bear back home.

Back we went to the zoo again, armed with the superintendent's letter. Bruno was driven into a small cage and hoisted on top of the car; the cage was tied securely, and a slow and careful return journey back home was accomplished.

Once home, a squad of workers were engaged for special work around our yard. An island was made for Bruno. It was twenty feet long and fifteen feet wide, and was surrounded by a dry moat, six feet wide and seven feet deep. A wooden box that once housed fowls was brought and put on the island for Bruno to sleep in at night. Straw was placed inside to keep him warm, and his 'baby', the gnarled stump, along with his 'gun', the piece of bamboo, both of which had been sentimentally preserved since he had been sent away to the zoo, were put back for him to play with. In a few days the workers hoisted the cage on to the island and Bruno was released. He was delighted; standing on his hind legs, he pointed his 'gun' and cradled his 'baby'. My wife spent hours sitting on a chair there while he sat on her lap. He was fifteen months old and pretty heavy too!

4. Which word from the passage describes "a keeper or custodian of a collection"?

   Ⓐ superintendent
   Ⓑ squad
   Ⓒ curator
   Ⓓ worker

5. Which word from the passage describes "a high-ranking official" or "someone who manages an organization"?

   Ⓐ superintendent
   Ⓑ squad
   Ⓒ curator
   Ⓓ worker

Week 7 Online Activity

Login to the Lumos student account and complete the following activities.

1. Reading assignment
2. Vocabulary practice
3. Write your summer diary

If you haven't created your Lumos account, use the URL and access code below to get started.
URL: http://www.lumoslearning.com/a/tedbooks
Access Code: G7-8MLSLH-19562

Day 36

1. If Robbie flips a quarter twice, what is the sample space for the possible outcomes?

   Ⓐ HT, HH, TT, TH
   Ⓑ HT, TH
   Ⓒ HT, TT, TH
   Ⓓ HH, TT

2. If Bret rolls a six-sided die twice, which table shows the sample space for possible outcomes?

Ⓐ

	1	2	3	4	5	6
1	1, 1	1, 2	1, 3	1, 4	1, 5	1, 6
2	2, 1	2, 2	2, 3	2, 4	2, 5	2, 6
3	3, 1	3, 2	3, 3	3, 4	3, 5	3, 6
4	4, 1	4, 2	4, 3	4, 4	4, 5	4, 6
5	5, 1	5, 2	5, 3	5, 4	5, 5	5, 6
6	6, 1	6, 2	6, 3	6, 4	6, 5	6, 6

Ⓒ

	1	2	3	4	5	6
1		1, 2	1, 3	1, 4	1, 5	1, 6
2	2, 1		2, 3	2, 4	2, 5	2, 6
3	3, 1	3, 2		3, 4	3, 5	3, 6
4	4, 1	4, 2	4, 3		4, 5	4, 6
5	5, 1	5, 2	5, 3	5, 4		5, 6
6	6, 1	6, 2	6, 3	6, 4	6, 5	

Ⓑ

	1	2	3	4	5	6
1	1, 1					
2		2, 2				
3			3, 3			
4				4, 4		
5					5, 5	
6						6, 6

Ⓓ

	1	2	3	4
1	1, 1	1, 2	1, 3	1, 4
2	2, 1	2, 2	2, 3	2, 4
3	3, 1	3, 2	3, 3	3, 4
4	4, 1	4, 2	4, 3	4, 4
5	5, 1	5, 2	5, 3	5, 4
6	6, 1	6, 2	6, 3	6, 4

3. There are three colors of stones in a bag: red, green, and blue. Two stones are drawn out at random (one at a time). What are the possible outcomes in which exactly one blue stone might be drawn?

   Ⓐ BR, GB BG
   Ⓑ BG, BR, BB
   Ⓒ RB, GB, BR, BG
   Ⓓ BG, BR

Day 36

For years, Sam had dreamed of being the best tennis player in the world. He went to tennis practice every single morning, and every single night. He spent every summer at tennis camp, and he gave up long weekends at the beach to work on his game. Now, it seemed his hard work was finally paying off: He was invited to try out for the state tennis team!

Still, there was something that was bothering Sam. The tryouts for the tennis team were on the same day as his mom's birthday, and he knew his family was planning a huge surprise party for her. He didn't want to hurt his mom's feelings by missing the party, but he also didn't want to miss his one shot at being a champion tennis player. He was in a quandary; he didn't know what to do.

For days, Sam went to bed worrying about the decision. If he went to the tryout, he worried he would seem selfish. If he stayed home, he would miss his one big shot at making the state team. In fact, despite the honor of being invited to try out, he hadn't even told his family about the opportunity. He was so stressed about making the decision of whether to go or not that he couldn't even think about sharing the news.

Weeks went by, and Sam was making no progress. Every day his coach asked him if he was ready for the tryout, and Sam couldn't even respond. Finally, Sam couldn't bear the stress any longer. He decided to talk to his grandfather about his predicament.

"You know, your mom wants you to be happy," he told Sam. "It would be a great birthday present for her to know you are making your dream come true."

Sam had never thought of it that way before, and after talking to his grandfather, he knew what he had to do. He immediately went home and sat down with his parents to let them know about the opportunity to try out for the state team. When Sam apologetically told his parents what day the tryouts were, they were so busy shrieking with excitement that he thought maybe they hadn't heard.

"But Mom, that means I'm going to miss your birthday," Sam said. "I am happy you are being so nice about it, but I still feel really bad."

"Are you kidding?" his mom asked? "This is the best present I could ask for!"

4. Which of the following is **NOT** a sign that Sam's parents raised him well?

Ⓐ He understood that family and tennis were both priorities he needed to balance in his life.
Ⓑ He sought guidance from his grandfather instead of running from the problem.
Ⓒ He knew that to become a great tennis player he had to put in a lot of hard work.
Ⓓ Sam didn't care about missing the party.

Fairy Tales by A Brothers' Grimm

A certain king once fell ill and the doctor declared that only a sudden fright would restore him to health, but the king was not a man for anyone to play tricks on, except his fool. One day, when the fool was with him in his boat, he cleverly pushed the king into the water. Help had already been arranged and the king was drawn ashore and put to bed. The fright, the bath and the rest in bed cured the diseased king.

The king wanted to frighten the fool for his act so he told him that he would be put to death. He directed the executioner privately not to use the axe but to let fall a single drop of water on the fool's neck. Amidst shouts and laughter, the fool was asked to rise and thank the king for his kindness.
But the fool never move; he was dead; killed by the master's joke.

5. What trick did the fool plan to cure the king?

Ⓐ a lot of medicines
Ⓑ injections
Ⓒ the sudden push into the water
Ⓓ the ride in the boat

Day 37

1. If 20% of applicants for a job are female, what is the probability that the first two applicants will be male?

   Ⓐ 64%
   Ⓑ 80%
   Ⓒ 60%
   Ⓓ 52%

2. If you want to simulate a random selection from a large population that is 40% adult and 60% children, how can you use slips of paper to do so?

   Ⓐ Make 5 slips of paper, 2 for adults and 3 for children. Randomly select slips of paper from the 5 to represent the choice of someone from the population.
   Ⓑ Make 2 slips of paper, 1 for adults and 1 for children. Randomly select slips of paper from the 2 to represent the choice of someone from the population.
   Ⓒ Make 100 slips of paper, 50 for adults and 50 for children. Randomly select slips of paper from the 100 to represent the choice of someone from the population.
   Ⓓ Make 3 slips of paper, 1 for adults and 2 for children. Randomly select slips of paper from the 3 to represent the choice of someone from the population.

3. A sandwich shop has 6 breads and 5 meats available for sandwiches. What is the probability that two people in a row will choose the same combination of bread and meat?

   Ⓐ 1 out of 11
   Ⓑ 1 out of 2
   Ⓒ 1 out of 30
   Ⓓ 1 out of 20

Use Those Clues – Make an Inference (RL.7.1)

Best Friends to Boyfriend/Girlfriend

Ever since they were kids, Julie and Max had been best friends. They went to kindergarten together. They went to summer camp together, They hung out together every weekend. But suddenly, things between the two had started to change.

Max had started playing on the football team and didn't have much time for Julie anymore. He was always busy, and he never seemed to make it to study hall, where the two used to swap stories about their favorite (or least favorite) teachers. In class, Julie noticed that Max never seemed to have his homework done on time anymore. She even noticed that he got a D on his last paper. She knew something was going on with him – but what?

At first, Julie decided to play it cool and see how things went. She tried waiting in the hall for Max after class to see if she could ask if he was OK. But days went by, and he never had time to stop. He'd rush right past her in the hall, only to leave her feeling even worse about what was happening between them.

Even though she wasn't sure she could handle the situation herself, Julie didn't want to talk to her parents because she was afraid they would tell her not to hang out with Max anymore. She barely saw him as it was, so she knew it would just make things worse if her parents didn't approve of him. She didn't want to tell Max's parents either because she didn't want him to get in trouble. Still, it seemed like something needed to change. Julie decided to go to one of her school counselors and let her know she was concerned.

When she walked into Mrs. Smith's room, she was surprised to see that Max was already sitting there.

"I'm sorry, I'll come back," Julie said.

"No, stay," said Max. "Maybe you can help."

Julie was surprised to find that Max had visited the counselor's office for the same reason she had: He was starting to feel overwhelmed with all of the things he was supposed to be doing as a student, an athlete and a friend. He needed some guidance on how to determine what truly mattered, and how to divide his time between all of the things that were important to him. When she realized that Max was still the same old Max (just a little more stressed), Julie was relieved. She was also happy to know that he had come to the conclusion on his own, without her having to talk to someone else about it. She decided it was a sign they were both growing up.

4. What can you infer about relationship between Julie and Max?

Ⓐ They were best of friends who cared about each other.
Ⓑ They really hated each other, so they went to the counselor alone.
Ⓒ They were just acquaintances who only occasionally talked.
Ⓓ They were neighbors.

From "The Dog and the Wolf" by Marmaduke Park

A wolf there was, whose scanty fare
Had made his person lean and spare;
A dog there was, so amply fed,
His sides were plump and sleek; 'tis said
The wolf once met this prosp'rous cur,
And thus began: "Your servant, sir;
I'm pleased to see you look so well,
Though how it is I cannot tell;
I have not broke my fast to-day;
Nor have I, I'm concern'd to say,
One bone in store or expectation,
And that I call a great vexation."

4. Which of the following can be inferred about the dog based on this passage?

Ⓐ That the dog was a golden retriever
Ⓑ That the dog had a caring master
Ⓒ That the dog was tall
Ⓓ That the dog belonged to the king

Week 8 Online Activity

Login to the Lumos student account and complete the following activities.

1. Reading assignment
2. Vocabulary practice
3. Write your summer diary

If you haven't created your Lumos account, use the URL and access code below to get started.
URL: http://www.lumoslearning.com/a/tedbooks
Access Code: G7-8MLSLH-19562

Answer Key & Detailed Explanations

Question No.	Answer	Detailed Explanation
1	C	3/2 is the constant of proportionality when y = 4 and x = 6. To find the constant of proportionality, apply the concept of unit rate. Since y is proportional to x, that means for every 6 of x, there is 4 of y. Simplifying the ratio 6/4 = 3/2.
2	A	First, find out how much cereal John eats in 8 days: (1) 3 bowls per day x 8 days = 24 bowls. Since it takes 2 gallons of milk to eat 24 bowls of cereal, set up the ratio and simplify: (2) 2/24 (GCF is 2, so divide numerator and denominator to find simplest form) (3) 1/12 Therefore, John uses 1/12 of a gallon of milk in each bowl of cereal.
3	C	In order to solve this problem, multiply 3/4 × 1/2 and then multiply the product times 1/2 in order to find the amount of milk used for each section of the cake. (1) 3/4 × 1/2 = 3/8 (2) 3/8 × 1/2 = 3/16 The amount of milk used is 3/4 + 3/8 + 3/16. (3) 3/4 + 3/8 + 3/16 -- The LCD is 16, so rename 3/4 (multiply both numerator and denominator by 4) and 3/8 (multiply both numerator and denominator by 2). (4) 12/16 + 6/16 + 3/16 = (5) 18/16 + 3/16 = (6) 21/16 (convert the improper fraction into a mixed number) (7) 1 5/16 Therefore, one and five-sixteenths cups of milk would be used to make the cake.
4	B	Answer choice two is the best answer. This answer is the best one because it shows that there were so many footprints that the policeman could not figure out exactly which prints belonged to the thief and which prints belonged to other customers. The first answer is incorrect because if the prints were marked, there would be no point in searching for the thief. The third answer choice can't be correct because the story clearly tells the reader that there are several footprints. The last answer choice does not make sense. Why would someone clean the footprints when a crime had been committed?
5	C	Answer choice three is correct. The first two choices are not mentioned in the story, so they cannot be the correct choice. The last answer choice is not the best choice. Although his mom is encouraging, she did not help him make the decision.

Day 2

Question No.	Answer	Detailed Explanation
1	B	In each case, if we multiply a by 3, we get b. b = 3a is the correct answer.
2	C	length/width = 3 / 2 =x / 4 2x = 12 x = 6 in. 6 in. is the correct answer.
3	D	Since the table shows that f = 5e, then 5 is the constant of proportionality. Therefore, f = 5e; so if e = 11, f = 55. 55 is the correct answer.
4	C	Answer choice three is correct. The quote indicates that the cabby was not paying attention, lost in thought, or asleep when the policemen called to him. It is meant to explain how the day had been slow, boring and cold, and he was somewhat startled and had a hard time getting his senses together to drive the policeman.
5	D	Answer choice four is correct. The bear behaved very differently when he went to the zoo. He would not eat and he lost weight. He was a happy bear before going to the zoo. His changed behavior was a clue that he was depressed.

Day 3

1	A	The line passes through the origin, so it is a proportional relationship. The second point gives the constant of proportionality, which is the y value divided by the x value: 3/5
2	C	For any of the pairs of data, divide the total cost by the number of tickets to find how much one ticket costs. For example, $21/3 = $7 per ticket.
3	B	For any of the pairs of data, divide the total cost by the number of pounds of seed to find how much one pound costs. For example, $17.50/10 = $1.75 per pound.

Question No.	Answer	Detailed Explanation
4	B	Answer choice two is the correct answer. The bear would not eat, and he was getting too thin. Then the wife came to see him, and he ate again.
5	B	Answer choice two is the correct answer. The bear and the wife were so close that both of them were not happy/healthy when they were separated.

Day 4

1	B	Divide the total cost by the number of hats: 18/3 = 6. This gives the cost per hat, which is the constant of proportionality in the equation: C = 6n.
2	A	Choose a pair of data. Divide the value of y by the value of x: 14/1 = 14. This gives the constant of proportionality in the equation: y = 14x.
3	D	Divide the total cost by the number of months: 100/4 = 25. This gives the cost per month, which is the constant of proportionality in the equation: C = 25m.
4	A	Answer choice one is the correct answer. The entire story is about the angst a young man feels when he worries about disappointing his mom. Family values and doing what is important (not missing a party) is the theme.
5	C	The story is about how Sam's open communication with his grandfather and later with his mother, helped in solving his dilemma and also strengthened his relationships with them. Hence, answer choice three is correct.

Question No.	Answer	Detailed Explanation
1	B	A straight line graph is a proportion if and only if it passes through the origin, (0, 0).
2	A	The unit rate is the amount per single unit of something. This means that the point located at 1 on the x-axis will indicate the unit rate: (1, 1).
3	D	Find the unit rate, which is the number of students per one class, by dividing the y value by the x value for the given point: 45/3 = 15 students per class.
4	A	Answer choice one is the correct answer. The cab driver indicates that his son was ill and then died. The story describes him sitting very still and somewhat dazed.
5	B	Answer choice number two is the correct answer. The cab driver's son died, and due to that he was grief stricken and sad. He was confused and not sure where to go with the policeman. He was sad (lamented) about the death of his child.

Day 6

1	D	In a set of equivalent ratios, or a proportion, the numerator and denominator of one ratio will be multipled by the same number to get the values of the other ratio. In this case, the denominator of the first ratio, 7, is multiplied by 3 to get to 21. This means (-3) must also be multiplied by 3 to get to (-9).
2	A	To find the constant of proportionality, find the relationship between p and s. When p = 10 and s = 2, dividing p by s shows that p is 5 times s. Therefore, the equation that shows the constant of proportionality is p = 5s.
3	B	To solve this proportion for x, multiply both sides of the equation by 54, and simplify the result.

Question No.	Answer	Detailed Explanation
4	A	Answer choice one is the correct answer. The first line in the story tells the reader where it is taking place.
5	C	Answer choice three is the correct answer. Snow is not common everywhere, but where it does on a regular basis, it is a winter form of precipitation.

Day 7

1	C	To find the answer, we need to represent each picture as a ratio of shaded parts to the total number of parts. We can see that only in the case of Option C, the fraction 4/8 reduces to 1/2. hence, Option C is the correct answer.
2	B	Remember: adding and subtracting rational numbers works just like integers. If you need to carry or borrow, the rules remain the same. 25 + 2.005 - 7.253 - 2.977 27.005 - 7.253 - 2.977 19.752 - 2.977 = 16.775
3	A	-3 4/5 + 9 7/10 - 2 11/20 = -3 16/20 + 9 14/20 - 2 11/20 -5 27/20 + 9 14/20 = -5 27/20 + 8 34/20 3 7/20 is the correct answer.
4	B	Answer choice two is the correct answer. The passage states, "But because of the neighborhoods' and our renters' children, poor Bruno, had to be kept chained most of the time." explains why the answer is the correct answer.
5	D	Answer choice number four is the best answer. All three of the other choices in the passage are mentioned as being things causing Max stress.

Day 8

1	A	The fact that p + q is less than p tells us that q is negative. p + q is exactly 1/3 less than p means, p + q = p - 1/3. Therefore, q is –1/3.

Question No.	Answer	Detailed Explanation
2	C	Anytime that you add a number and its opposite, the sum is always 0.
3	B	The difference between 12/5 and 4/5 will be the value of q. The difference is 8/5.
4	C	Answer choice three is the best answer. The words to describe their habitats are fun and non-sensical (Sofsky-Popsky and Pipple Popple). This helps sets the tone of silly. There is no indication of greed or really of constant hunger. And whether the animals are diverse or not does not answer the question about tone.
5	B	Answer choice two is the best answer. "Thus the man became rich and lived on with his wife and children. And that child, that came to him in his sleep, was an angel sent by the Lord God, whose will it was to aid the poor man, and to reveal secrets which had not been revealed till then." describes a happy, relieved, and JOYFUL feeling. There is no anger, or confusion in this passage's end, nor any seriousness.

Day 9

Question No.	Answer	Detailed Explanation
1	A	Both terms inside of the parentheses are being subtracted, and subtraction of a number is the same as addition of its opposite.
2	C	The distance between two points can be found by taking the absolute value of the difference of the two points.
3	B	Because Kyle and Mark traveled in opposite directions, let one of their distances be a negative value. The distance between the two of them is the absolute value of the difference of their positions, which is 8 when evaluated.
4	A	Part of the definition of a villanelle is that it have two rhyming patterns. This poem has two rhyming patterns so answer choice number one is the answer to select.
5	D	In poetry repetition is used to stress an idea, sound or feeling. The word me is not repeated, so answer choice number four is the best answer.

Question No.	Answer	Detailed Explanation
1	A	The commutative property states that parts of an addition statement can be written in any order and the same sum will result.
2	C	The 92 can be written as 82 + 10, so that the 10 and 8 can first be subtracted, and then the result can be added to 82.
3	B	The whole number parts can be added together, and the fraction parts can be added together, resulting in 11 and 12/8. The 12/8 part is a full 8/8, or 1, and an additional 4/8, so that we have 12 and 4/8, which simplifies to 12 and 1/2.
4	A	Answer choice one is the correct answer. The passage explains that the swindlers (dishonest people) told the Emperor that if a person was wise, and worthy of their job/status, they would be able to see the fabric/costumes. But, the men never intended to make any clothes. No one was willing to admit that they saw no clothes because they did not want to appear to be unworthy. It took a child, who did not know to hide what he saw, to point out the obvious. The remaining three answers describe the swindlers (2 and 3) and what an official thought upon seeing the "clothes." They do not answer the question: **why** did the Emperor agree to hire the men (swindlers).
5	A	Answer choice one is the best answer. The king is insecure about himself and that is why he hired the swindlers. He only cares about looks and he wanted a "trick" to help him with his work/people. The minister would be considered wise and trustworthy, so if he could not see the fabric, he would be out of a job. Not seeing the fabric made him feel as though maybe he really wasn't good enough for the job. Choice two is incorrect because the minister never indicated he wanted to fool the public. Choice three is incorrect because only the Emperor was worried about clothes. And answer four is incorrect. The Emperor thought the minister could see things not visible. The Emperor never claimed to.

Question No.	Answer	Detailed Explanation
1	A	Remember that when we multiply like signs, either (- * -) or (+ * +), the result is positive, and when we multiply unlike signs, the result is negative. Since we are multiplying some number by - 9 and get +36, we know that the sign of the unknown quantity is also negative. Now, 4 * 9 = 36; so - 4 * - 9 = 36. - 4 is the correct answer.
2	D	This problem requires the use of the distributive property. We must distribute the quantity outside parentheses to each term inside parentheses. - 2(a + 3b) = - 2a - 6b. - 2a - 6b is the correct answer.
3	C	In order to solve 1/2 ÷ 2/3. Keep the first fraction, change the division symbol into a multiplication symbol, and flip the second fraction before solving the problem. (1) 1/2 ÷ 2/3 = (2) 1/2 × 3/2 = (3) (1 × 3)/(2 × 2) = (4) 3/4 3/4 is the correct answer.
4	C	Answer choice three is the best answer. The dream predicted what the man should do, and when he did this, his life improved.
5	A	Answer choice one is the correct answer. The boy was very serious and quiet. He hardly spoke or did anything.

Day 12

1	A	0 cannot be the divisor in a division problem. 0 cannot be the divisor in a division problem because division by 0 is undefined.
2	B	Dividing a negative number by a negative number results in a positive number. If only one of the dividend or divisor is negative, then the quotient is negative.
3	C	Divide the length of the trail by the length of one leg, and the number of legs results: 8.

Question No.	Answer	Detailed Explanation
4	A	The first answer choice is the best choice. The first line of the second stanza tells the reader what Revere was planning to do.
5	B	Answer choice two. The first line of the second paragraph states why Revere was riding.

Day 13

1	A	Multiply the 3 by the numerator, 1, and then divide by the denominator 3. The result is 1.
2	C	The commutative property states that multiplication can be done in any order and the same product will result.
3	B	Dividing by a fraction is the same thing as multiplying by the reciprocal of that fraction. Multiply, then, by 2 rather than dividing by 1/2: 4 x 2 = 8.
4	B	Answer choice two is correct. Choice one describes how Verdi felt about the organ and man in town, and choices three and four talk about the spinet being fixed. Only choice two references how much he enjoyed practicing – so much so that he wore it out.
5	D	The answer choice four is correct. The other choices talk about what skunks eat, but choice four specifically discusses how much they eat.

Day 14

1	C	Divide 7 by 8 using long division, and the result is 0.875.
2	A	Divide 5 by 6 using long division. The decimal repeats endlessly: 0.83333…
3	A	If the decimal terminates, then the number can always be written as the quotient of two integers and is rational.

Question No.	Answer	Detailed Explanation
4	B	All answer choices seem to be correct, but the best answer is the second choice. The article does discuss fall weather and trees, but it does not <u>focus</u> on weather. Also, the point is not the life cycle of TREES, but the process of the leaves turning in the fall and dropping from the trees.
5	C	Answer choice three is the best answer. The first choice is only about winter sports. The second answer is closer to what the article is about, however the third answer is BEST. The last answer is not appropriate. Popular Sports is too broad. The article was about a specific sporting event that is extremely old, so the third answer choice is the most accurate.

Day 15

1	B	$15.00 - $9.39 = $15.00 - $ 9.39 $ 5.61 is the correct answer.
2	B	50.75 x 25 = 1268.75 pounds 1268.75 pounds is the correct answer.
3	A	1528.80 pounds ÷ 50 bags = 30.576 pounds in each bag. 30.576 is the correct answer.
4	C	Answer choice number three is the best answer. The relationship is causal, or an "acquaintance" in nature. There is nothing about being related, and they are not enemies, no anger exists. Also, they are not best friends, or the question would not need to be asked. The BEST answer is the third, They know one another, but they don't fully "get" each other.
5	A	The best answer choice is the first one. The ant was hard at work preparing for the future, and had he stopped to visit with the grasshopper he would have not been prepared.

Day 16

1	A	Remember: "Younger than" is a key phrase that will indicate subtraction. If A is the age of Ruby's brother, and she is 2 years younger than her brother, the correct expression is A - 2.

Question No.	Answer	Detailed Explanation
2	C	$8n - (3n-6) = 8n - 3n + 6 = 5n + 6$ $5n + 6$ is the correct answer.
3	A	$6t + (3t - 5) =$ Remove parentheses: $6t + (3t - 5) = 6t + 3t - 5$. Now combine like terms: $6t + 3t - 5 = 9t - 5$ $9t - 5$ is the correct answer.
4	C	Answer choice number three is the best answer. All three answer choices, except the third, are true about the substance. All three are mentioned in the passage. The best answer is the substance is safe for animals. This cannot be true because it is intended to get rid of rodents and it made Bruno very ill.
5	A	Answer choice one is the best selection. The passage says spinet, like a small piano. This indicates the instrument is like a piano. The passage implies the story takes place prior to electricity being common, so choice four is incorrect. Trumpet and violin are instruments, but not like an organ or piano.

Day 17

1	C	A percent is a ratio that compares a number to 100. Therefore, 5% is 5 out of 100. To convert a percent to a decimal, divide by 100: $5 \div 100 = 0.05$. To find 5% of a number, multiply the number times the decimal form of 5%: $0.05n$. $0.05n$ is the correct answer.
2	C	$SP = RP - 0.15(RP)$ $SP = RP(1 - 0.15)$ $SP = RP(0.85)$ $SP = 0.85RP$ is the correct answer.
3	D	$P = l + w + l + w$ Combine like terms. $P = 2(l) + 2(w)$ Factor out 2. $P = 2(l + w)$ is the correct answer.
4	A	Answer choice one is the best answer. Each paragraph covers a different aspect of the life of the Bushmen. Answer choice two is not at all reasonable. The passage does not narrow down to one aspect. Answer choice three is incorrect because the passage is not organized in the order something happened. Answer four is incorrect too because there is nothing to compare. This is an informative passage.

Question No.	Answer	Detailed Explanation
5	A	Answer choice one is the best answer to the question. The second answer is part of the passage, but does not address the question asked. The last two answer choices are in the passage, but they are not "sections" that would answer the question.

Day 18

1	D	The first step to solving this problem is to figure out the value of t, the number of hours. As you know, 7 am to 3 pm represents 5 hours to 12 pm, then another 3 hours to 3pm, for a total of 8 hours. This gives us W = 3.75(8) = 30, a full tank.
2	D	Let the volume of water = w and volume of milk = m. m 3 = w 8 Rearranging the above equation, m = 3w/8 m + w = 187 cubic ft. Replacing the value of m by 3w/8 in the above equation, 3w/8 + w = 187 11w/8 = 187 w = (187*8)/11 w = 136 cubic ft.
3	D	Remember: The volume of a rectangular box is V = lwh. This lets us set up the following equation: 960 = 12(10)h 960 = 120h 8 = h This gives us a height of 8 inches, as indicated.
4	A	Answer choice number one is the best one. The other three answers are not positive or encouraging. The first choice is positive of Verdi.
5	B	Answer choice number two is the best answer. The author describes the Czar's personality and discusses what others thought of him. The author mentions the Czar's gentleness and desire to not be so firm as his father, yet most of the people did not understand this, so he was not well thought of. The author feels the Czar was trying to do well and was misunderstood.

Day 19

1	A	In order to find out how much Bill should charge his client, divide 130 by 4, and then add the quotient to 130: (1) 130 ÷ 4 = 32.50 (2) 130 + 32.50 = $162.50

Question No.	Answer	Detailed Explanation
2	C	First, write the expressions based on the language in the problem: length = 6x width = (1/3)(6x) height = (1/2)(6x) Next, solve for x based on the formula for volume, lwh. (1) $6x \times ((1/3)(6x)) \times ((1/2)(6x)) = 972$ (2) $6x \times 2x \times 3x = 972$ (3) $12x^2 \times 3x = 972$ (4) $36x^3 = 972$ (divide each side by 36) (5) $x^3 = 27$ (6) $x = 3$
3	D	Let x be the width of the rectangular backyard. Length = 2x. Perimeter of the backyard = $x + 2x + x + 2x = 180$ ft. $6x = 180$ ft. $x = 180 / 6 = 30$ ft. = width of the backyard. Length of the backyard = $2x = 60$ ft. Total length of the shrubbery Taylor needs to trim = width+length+length = $x + 2x + 2x = 150$ ft.
4	A	Answer choice one is correct. A time-lapse video of the leaves changing color may be included in a documentary to help someone understand how the leaves change color. Paintings are just representations, not the real thing, animals hibernating are an example given in the text but not helpful, and subtitles wouldn't do much more than the text itself.
5	C	Answer choice three is correct. A diagram of the process would be most helpful. The other three could be used to make it more entertaining or to add minor details.

Day 20

1	C	3000 must be multiplied by y, the years of experience. This amount must then be added to the base salary of $50,000. This sum must be less than or equal to $70,000.
2	B	The weekly increase of 45 is multiplied by the number of weeks. This amount is added to the initial savings of 225. This sum must be greater than or equal to 500.
3	D	The number of minutes of charging time must be multiplied by 2 and divided by 3 to find the percentage of the battery that is charged over that time. This is then added to the initial charge of 20 percent, and the sum must be at least 75.

Question No.	Answer	Detailed Explanation
4	C	Answer choice three is correct. A scientist should present the information without any slant or bias to a specific belief or cause. A journalist might want to tell a story with more exciting aspects to get viewers, a student might not know enough facts and information to be completely accurate, and an activist might have a cause they want focus on, so they might not be as fair at the information as a scientist should be.
5	C	Answer choice three is correct. One could interview the author, but what if he/she did not research properly? Reading an encyclopedia is a good start, but the historian who specializes in Egypt would be the best source for verifying the information. Going to Egypt might be fun, but that would not necessarily tell the reader if the information in the article is factual.

Question No.	Answer	Detailed Explanation
1	D	Remember: In order to solve a similarity question, set up a proportion with corresponding sides, and solve!: x/12 = 35/15 or x/12 = 21/9 You can use cross products (ad = bc) to solve for x. (1) x/12 = 35/15 (2) 15x = (35)(12) (3) 15x = 420 (4) x = 420 ÷ 15 (5) x = 28
2	A	If the similarity ratio is 3/2, then the ratio of the areas is the square of that ratio: 3/2 × 3/2 = 9/4.
3	A	In order to solve a similarity problem, set up a proportion with corresponding sides: 8/4 = 16/8. Both ratios in simplest form are 2/1. Therefore, the similarity ratio is 2/1.
4	C	Answer choice number three is the correct selection. If someone had been able to intervene, it would have helped the victim in the first passage. The other three answers are good answers in general, but the third answer best fits the situation of the boy in passage A.
5	A	Answer choice one is the correct answer. The first passage tells an incident, the second passage is informational. They are both about bullying, but from a different genre.

Question No.	Answer	Detailed Explanation
1	D	The sum of any two sides of a triangle is always greater than the third side. Here, the sum of 1 + 1 = 2. Since the sum of 1 + 1 is not greater than 2, the lengths given cannot be the side lengths of a triangle.
2	C	The sum of any two sides of a triangle is always greater than the third side. Here, the sum of 4 + 8.5 = 12.5. Since the sum of 4 + 8.5 is not greater than 14, the lengths given cannot be the side lengths of a triangle.

Question No.	Answer	Detailed Explanation
3	A	The sum of the measure of angles in a triangle is always 180°. To find a missing angle, add the known angles and subtract the sum from 180°. (1) 100 + 60 = 160 (2) 180 - 160 = 20. Therefore, the measure of the third angle is 20°.
4	A	Answer choice one is correct. There is no subject but there is a verb, so this is a phrase. A phrase is a meaningful group of words which may appear to contain either a subject OR a verb--but NOT both. A phrase can NOT stand alone as a sentence. A clause is a meaningful group of words which contains a subject and a verb. There are two types of clauses: 1) independent and 2) dependent. http://www.csus.edu/owl/index/sent/clause_quiz.htm
5	C	Answer choice three is correct. An independent clause contains all of the parts of a complete sentence: a subject, verb and a complete thought.

Day 23

Question No.	Answer	Detailed Explanation
1	C	A cylinder has two circular bases and one curved surface that appears as a rectangle when the cylinder is shown as a net. Therefore, a horizontal cross section would show a circle.
2	A	A prism consists of two congruent bases and various congruent faces; therefore, the cross sections of a prism must show congruent polygons.
3	A	In order to form a cube, the nets must fold together to make the shape. Here, the figure would not form a cube when folded together to make a three-dimensional figure.
4	A	Answer choice one is correct. Everybody is a singular subject, so it requires a verb that ends in -s.
5	B	Answer choice two is correct. Subjects and verbs must match in number (number of items in the subject) and person (1st, 2nd or 3rd). In this sentence the subject, "car", is singular and third person. The verb "needs" is also singular, third person.

Day 24

Question No.	Answer	Detailed Explanation
1	C	The correct answer is 90°. Selecting 25° results from incorrectly applying the qualities of a circle graph to the circle (a whole circle represents 100%, so four equal parts equal 25% each). Choosing 180° is a result of measuring the angle of the line formed by dividing the circle into two equal parts (a straight line measures 180°). A circle measures 360°, so the measure of each angle formed at the center would be less than 360°. By dividing it into 4 equal pieces, each angle will be $360 \div 4 = 90°$.
2	C	The correct answer is 50.2 cm². To find the area of a circle, apply the formula $A = \pi r^2$. Since the problem gives the diameter of the circle, the first step is to find the radius by dividing the diameter by 2. $8 \div 2 = 4$ cm. Next, plug in the numbers into the formula: (1) $\pi 4^2 =$ (2) $3.14 \times 4^2 =$ (3) $3.14 \times 16 =$ (4) 50.24 cm² (5) 50.2 cm² (rounded to the nearest tenth). Common errors made when applying the area formula to circles are multiplying the radius by 2 instead of by itself (which would result in 25.1 cm²) or using the diameter of the circle to find the area (resulting in 201.0 cm²).
3	C	The correct answer is 20 cm. To find the radius when given the circumference of the circle, use $C/(2\pi)$, where C equals circumference. Insert the numbers from the problem, and solve: (1) $r = C/(2\pi)$ (2) $125 \div (2 \times 3.14) =$ (3) $125 \div 6.28 =$ (4) 19.90 cm = (5) 20 cm (rounded to the nearest whole number). Finding a radius of 19 cm results from rounding down instead of rounding up. An answer of 10 cm results from dividing the radius by 2. Choosing 24 cm is based on adding $2 + \pi$ and dividing 125 by the sum.
4	B	Answer choice two is the correct answer. An adverb ends in -ly. The fact that the computer is older tells the reader that it is probably not very fast or effective. So, it cannot be quickly. Fast is not appropriate due to the meaning and form of the word. Angrily does not apply to the computer's connection. It might to the computer operator, but not the actual machine.

Question No.	Answer	Detailed Explanation
5	B	Answer choice two is the correct answer. When two adjectives appear next to one another, they should be separated by a comma. It is similar to the listing rule of comma usage.

Day 25

Question No.	Answer	Detailed Explanation
1	D	The answer is 100°. Reminder: Angles that together form a straight line are called supplementary, meaning they add to 180 degrees. In this case, 50 + x + 30 = 180 requires an x value of 100 degrees.
2	C	The answer is 50° and 100°. Angles that together form a straight line are supplementary, meaning their measures add to 180 degrees. In this case, x + (x + 50) + 30 = 180 can only be satisfied by an x value of 50, resulting in angles of measure 50 and 100 degrees.
3	B	The answer is 77.5 degrees. When two lines intersect, they form vertical angles, which are equal in measure. Angle a and angle b are vertical angles. To find the value of angle b, divide 155 by 2. The quotient is the value of angle b: 155 ÷ 2 = 77.5 degrees.
4	A	Answer choice one is correct. Commas go between coordinate adjectives. Since you can place an "and" between fascinating and intelligent, they are coordinating adjectives.
5	B	Answer choice two is correct. Commas go between coordinate adjectives. Since you can place an "and" between slippery and dangerous, they are coordinate conjunctions.

Day 26

Question No.	Answer	Detailed Explanation
1	C	The answer is 27.09 square centimeters. To calculate the area of a rectangle, multiply the length and width. Multiplying 6.3 × 4.3 = 27.09 square centimeters. An answer of 10.5 square centimeters results from adding 6.2 + 4.3. Choosing 24 square centimeters is the result of rounding 6.2 and 4.3 to 6 and 4 before multiplying. Selecting 21 square centimeters results from adding 6.2 + 6.2 + 10.5 + 10.5.

Question No.	Answer	Detailed Explanation
2	D	The answer is 512 in^3. The formula for the volume for a cube is V = s^3, where s is the length of one side. Multiplying 8 × 8 × 8 = 512 in^3. An answer of 24 in^3 results from adding 8 + 8 + 8. Finding 64 in^3 is the result of using the area formula, s^2. Selecting 128 in^3 results from multiplying 8 x 8 x 2.
3	A	The correct answer is 15 square units. To find the correct answer, apply the formula for the area of a triangle, A = ½bh. First, calculate the base by adding 6 + 4 = 10. Next, multiply the base times the height: 10 × 3 = 30. Then, divide the product by 2: 30 ÷ 2 = 15 square units. Finding an answer of 30 square units results from multiplying the base times the height and not dividing the product by 2. Selecting 36 square units is the result of multiplying 4 × 6 to find the base, multiplying the base, 24, by the height, 3, and dividing the product by 2: 72 ÷ 2 = 36 Choosing 18 square units results from using 6 as the base, multiplying the base by 3, and not dividing the product by 2.
4	A	"Threw" is a homonym of "through" (the correct spelling for this case). "Threw" is the word that means the past tense of "to throw".
5	C	The correct spelling of this word is "experiment."

Day 27

1	C	A group of randomly selected students in the hallways would produce the least amount of bias because it is unlikely for assumptions to be made or factors that influence the data to be present. For example, students in the 8th grade may be taller than other students in other grades, skewing the data toward a higher average. A similar assumption can be made about students on the basketball team. Joe and Mary would already have an idea of the height of their friends.
2	A	A random, representative group represents the people to survey in a population because each person in the population has an equal chance of being included and there is less of a chance of bias altering the results of the survey.
3	C	As the size of the sample (people surveyed) increases, the results become more accurate. Therefore, increasing the sample size increases the reliability of the results.

Question No.	Answer	Detailed Explanation
4	C	Answer choice three is correct. All of the other choices are general. Choice three is more specific and precise.
5	D	Answer choice four is correct. Answer choices one and two are longer and more redundant. Answer choice three is better, but can still be cleaned up.

Day 28

1	B	A group of randomly selected strangers in different places of a mall would produce the least amount of bias because there is unlikely to be assumptions made or factors that influence the data.
2	A	In the survey, 83 students selected science as their favorite subject while the other subjects had a combined number of 94 students. Therefore, an inference can be made that students prefer science over the other subjects.
3	A	In the sample, a combined 93 students chose action movies, 41 students chose drama, and 73 chose comedy. Therefore, an inference can be made that students prefer action movies to other types of movies.
4	C	Answer choice three is correct. When someone finds themselves in a quandary, it is usually because they have to make a choice. This causes them to have to weigh the pros and cons of the decisions. The boy in this story has to make a decision, and it is causing him stress. He is in a quandary.
5	D	Bruno receives medicine through a shot injection. The answer choice is D. Also it is used as a noun in the story.

Question No.	Answer	Detailed Explanation
1	C	There is a strong positive correlation between the height and the weight because there is an upward trend in the weight as a person gets taller.
2	C	When analyzing the heights of the basketball players and soccer players, the average height of the basketball players is 5'4, and the average height of the soccer players is 5 1 1/2. Therefore, the average height of the basketball players is higher than the average height of the soccer players.
3	D	Remember: the mean represents the average of the values, which is calculated by adding all the values together then dividing by the number of values you added. In this case, (24 + 36 + 55 + 65) / 4 = 45, and (72 + 78) / 2 = 75. The difference between these two values is 30, as indicated.
4	C	Answer choice three is correct. Autonomous means to be in control of self.
5	B	Answer choice two is correct.

Day 30

1	B	Out of 16 scores, 13 of 16 are 4 or below. Since the majority of the scores are low, a person can infer that, overall, customers had a bad experience.
2	D	To answer this question, look at the results of the different dishes. Spaghetti: 7 Pizza: 13 Calzone: 9 Baked Ziti: 2 Since only 2 people said that baked ziti was their favorite food, it is the menu item the manager should remove from the menu.
3	A	The measures of central tendency are mean, which is the average of a set of data; median, which is the middle of a set of data, and mode, which is the value which appears most in a set of data.

Question No.	Answer	Detailed Explanation
4	B	Answer choice two is correct. To find the answer quickly, Jorge should look up the meaning in the glossary of the textbook.
5	C	Answer choice three is correct. Using a glossary or dictionary will get him the definition, but a thesaurus will provide similar words.

Day 31

1	D	Mary originally had 10 marbles in her bag. When she removed 3 marbles, she had 7 remaining marbles. Six of those marbles are yellow. Probability is: (chance of successful outcome)/(total number of outcomes). Plug in the numbers, and solve. 6 chances to pick yellow out of 7 outcomes = 6/7
2	A	There are four number 2 cards in a deck of 52. If one number 2 card is removed, that leaves three number 2 cards out of 51 cards. Probability is: (chance of successful outcome)/(total number of outcomes). Therefore, there is a 3 out of 51 chance that John will pick number 2 at random.
3	B	Maggie has a total of 46 coins, 6 of which are quarters. Probability is: (chance of successful outcome)/(total number of outcomes). Therefore, there is a 6 out of 46 chance that Maggie will pick a quarter. This simplifies to 3 out of 23.
4	D	A thesaurus is like a dictionary of synonyms. It is used to find alternate words that mean the same thing as a common word.
5	C	Manuals provide step-by-step directions for using different items such as software programs.

Day 32

1	C	Create a sample space by listing all the possible outcomes. For each coin flipped, it will land on heads or tails. Therefore, for two coins, there could be outcomes of (heads, heads), (heads, tails), (tails, heads), and (tails, tails).

Question No.	Answer	Detailed Explanation
2	A	When testing probability, larger samples (experiments) yield more accurate results. An experiment of 1,000 coin tosses could adequately test if a coin would land on its head 1/2 of the time (about 500 of 1,000).
3	D	Since there are three even numbers (2, 4, 6) and three odd numbers (1, 3, 5) on a six-sided die, the probability is 3 out of 6 for rolling either an even or an odd number. Therefore, it is equally likely to roll an even or odd number. There is also a 3 out of 6 chance of rolling a number from 1 to 3.
4	C	Answer choice three is correct. Bricks are heavy and 2000 pounds would be extremely heavy.
5	D	Answer choice four is the correct answer. Off the cuff usually means with no notes or talking points. The person just "does it."

Day 33

1	D	Remember: In a compound and event, you can multiply the probabilities of each event in order to arrive at a final solution. There is a 1/6 chance she will roll a 3 and a 1/6 chance Sara rolls a 5. This means there is a 1/6(1/6) = 1/36 chance she will roll both. Another way to approach this problem is to create the sample space containing all possible combinations. (B, Y): (1,1), (1,2), (1,3), (1,4), (1,5), (1,6) (2,1), (2,2), (2,3), (2,4), (2,5), (2,6) (3,1), (3,2), (3,3), (3,4), (3,5), (3,6) (4,1), (4,2), (4,3), (4,4), (4,5), (4,6) (5,1), (5,2), (5,3), (5,4), (5,5), (5,6) (6,1), (6,2), (6,3), (6,4), (6,5), (6,6) From this list it is clear that only one out of the 36 total possible matches the (3,5) described.
2	B	Probability is defined as chance that an event will occur (a number between 0 and 1). The closer a probability is to 1, the more likely it is to occur. Drawing a number line with marks 0.1 distance apart can help determine the likelihood of an event occurring. Since 0.91 is close to 1, it represents an event most likely to occur.
3	D	Probability is defined as the chance that an event will occur (a number from 0 to 1). Since 5/4 is a rational number greater than 1, it cannot represent a probability.

Question No.	Answer	Detailed Explanation
4	C	Homonyms are words that sound the same when they are pronounced, but that are spelled differently and usually have different meanings.
5	A	Synonyms are words that have similar meanings. They can usually replace each other in a sentence and the sentence will hold the same meaning.

Day 34

1	B	Because 5 of the 8 times it was flipped, the result was heads, the probability of heads is 5 out of 8.
2	A	If 20% of the rolls result in a 2, then 20% of 50 rolls would be (0.20)(50) = 10 times.
3	D	An even distribution of the odds and evens would be 25 each. 4 more odds would mean 27 odds and 23 evens.
4	B	Facetious is not generally used in a positive way.
5	A	Boot has negative connotations. It is not used in positive situations.

Day 35

1	B	For the t-shirt, polo shirt and sweater, determine how many outfits Jane can make counting the number of jeans and khakis and sneakers and sandals she can match with her shirts. Therefore, there are 12 combinations available for the outfits Jane can make.
2	C	For the t-shirt, polo shirt and sweater, determine how many outfits Jane can make, counting the number of jeans and khakis and sneakers and sandals she can match with her shirts. Therefore, there are 12 combinations available for the outfits Jane can make. For 12 outfits, there are 3 outfits with jeans and sneakers. Therefore, there is a 3 out of 12 probability that Jane will wear jeans and sneakers. 3 out of 12 is 3/12, which is 1/4 in simplest form.

Question No.	Answer	Detailed Explanation
3	C	For each name in first place, there are 24 ways the other names can be arranged. $24 \times 5 = 120$ ways. Alternate Method : First spot can be arranged in 5 ways. After selecting the first spot, second spot can be arranged in 4 ways and so on for the third, fourth and fifth spot. So Top five spots can be arranged in $5 \times 4 \times 3 \times 2 \times 1 = 120$ ways.
4	C	Answer choice three is correct. A curator is a keeper or custodian of a collection, such as the collection of animals at the zoo.
5	A	Answer choice one is correct. A superintendent is a high-ranking official or someone who manages the zoo.

Day 36

1	A	All possible combinations of heads (H) and tails (T) must be named; there are four such combinations.
2	A	All possible combinations of the numbers 1 through 6 must be given in the table. There are 36 different possible combinations.
3	D	The blue stone might be either the first or second of the stones. The other stone could be either red or green.
4	D	Answer choice four is the correct answer. Sam was very concerned about what his parents would think if he missed the party. This shows he considers other's feelings and is a sign he was raised well by his parents.
5	C	Answer choice three is correct. The answer is in the passage and can be found in the third paragraph. The first two choices are not mentioned in the story, and although they make sense for today, this passage does not indicate that was an option. The last choice is in the story, a ride in the boat, but what is expected to cure the king is a sudden fright (something unexpected), not a ride in a boat.

Question No.	Answer	Detailed Explanation
1	A	The probability that the first will be male is 80%. Multiply by 80% again to find the probability that the second is also male.
2	A	The slips of paper should be in the same ratio as the population, which can be done by 2 adult slips and 3 child slips.
3	C	The probability that the second customer will choose the same bread as the first is 1 in 6. The probability that he will choose the same meat is 1 in 5. Multiply these together to find the probability of choosing both.
4	A	Answer choice one is correct. They were very good friends/best friends. The passage explains their interactions with each other, indicating they were more than acquaintances or neighbors.
5	B	Answer choice two is the best answer. Because the dog was well fed, unlike the wolf, his master must have cared for the dog.

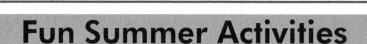

Fun Summer Activities

Learn Sign Language

What is American Sign Language?
American Sign Language (ASL) is a complete, complex language that employs signs made by moving the hands combined with facial expressions and postures of the body. It is the primary language of many North Americans who are deaf and is one of several communication options used by people who are deaf or hard-of-hearing.

Where did ASL originate?
The exact beginnings of ASL are not clear, but some suggest that it arose more than 200 years ago from the intermixing of local sign languages and French Sign Language (LSF, or Langue des Signes Française). Today's ASL includes some elements of LSF plus the original local sign languages, which over the years have melded and changed into a rich, complex, and mature language. Modern ASL and modern LSF are distinct languages and, while they still contain some similar signs, can no longer be understood by each other's users.

Source: https://www.nidcd.nih.gov/health/american-sign-language

Why should one learn sign language?

Enrich your cognitive skills: Sign language can enrich the cognitive development of a child. Since, different cognitive skills can be acquired as a child, learning sign language, can be implemented with practice and training in early childhood.

Make new friends: You could communicate better with the hearing-impaired people you meet, if you know the sign language, it is easier to understand and communicate effectively.

Volunteer: Use your ASL skills to interpret as a volunteer. volunteers can help in making a real difference in people's lives, with their time, effort and commitment.

Bilingual: If you are monolingual, here is an opportunity to become bilingual, with a cause.

Private chat: It would be useful to converse with a friend or in a group without anyone understanding, what you are up to.

Let's Learn the Alphabets

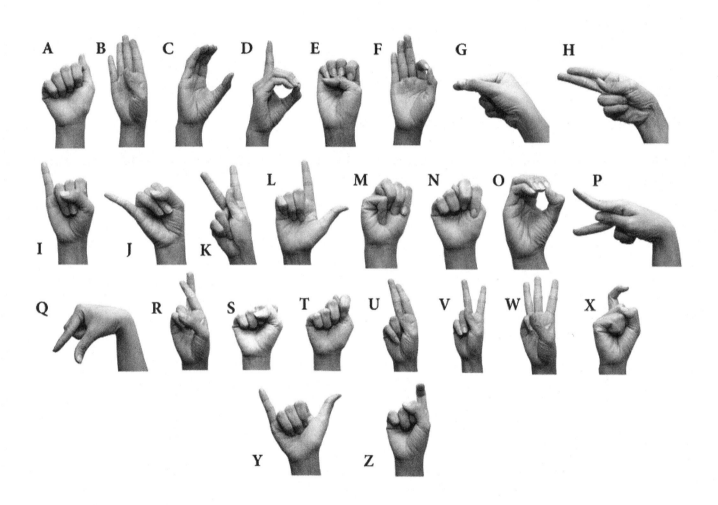

Sign language is fun if it is practiced with friends!
Partner with your friends or family members and try the following activities.

Activity

1. Communicate the following to your friend using the ASL.
   - USA
   - ASL

If your friend hasn't mastered the ASL yet, give the above alphabet chart to your friend.

2. Try saying your name in ASL using the hand gestures.

3. Have your friend communicate a funny word using ASL and you try to read it without the help of the chart. List the words you tried below.

Let's Learn the Numbers

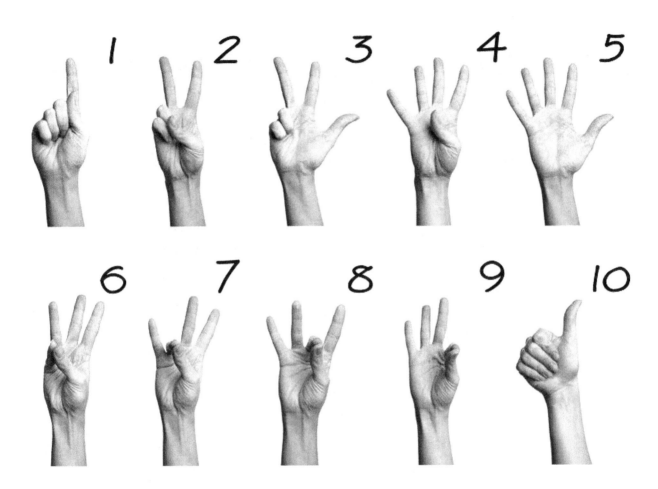

Activity:

1. Share your postal code through ASL to your friend.
2. Communicate your home phone number in ASL to your friend.

Let's Learn Some Words

RED

ORANGE

YELLOW

GREEN

PURPLE

BLUE

EAT

DRINK

MORE

PLEASE

THANK YOU

SORRY

Downhill Skiing: Seven Crucial Ways to Improve Your Skills on the Slopes

Downhill Skiing is a sport that requires keen balance, powerful leg strength, and a bit of courage -- to say the least.

When first starting out, it can be a bit daunting for beginners to know where to start; not to mention the fear of falling and getting hurt. This guide will help any novice Downhill skier to improve their skills and become more confident with their abilities on the mountain.

1. Improve Your Balance

As you might imagine, balance is a fundamental skill to have for any skier: if you can't balance well, you won't go far in the sport.

While you might be able to balance on one leg when standing, it is a completely different story when you are sliding down a hill with long planks attached to your boots.

Although it might not be the funniest thing to do, drills on flat ground or the "bunny hill" will help you improve your balance.

To start, you can try the "balance on one side drill", whereby you stand on one ski, lift your other foot off the ground, and propel yourself forward with your poles -- using what is called the double pull (pushing down on both poles simultaneously).

Do this for thirty seconds or so then switch legs. You'll find that over time, your stability will gradually improve.

2. Build Strength in your Upper Legs

The constant maneuvering necessary when skiing will make even the strongest legs feel like noodles. To last longer on the hills and become more powerful on the powder, you should strengthen your legs by doing squats.

Start standing with your feet shoulder-width apart. Let your body drop slowly while keeping your weight on your heels, your hips back, and your back straight and at a slight forward angle.

Continue as deep as you can, ensuring that your nose, knees, and toes are constantly in alignment. Do the reverse and push yourself back up, maintaining the same form, and repeat as many times as you can. Although your legs will burn, push past the pain for best results.

3. Increase your Calf Endurance

Calve-ups are a great way to make your calves more muscular. Simply find some stairs or a ledge and stand with heel hanging off the edge.

6 Ways to Become a Wake Board Whiz

1.   Relax and be Patient

Relaxing on the board helps you get a better center of gravity, which keeps you stable on the board. The more loose and relaxed you are, the better balance you will have. Bend your knees, stay low to the board, keep your arms straight and let the boat pull you. Focus on staying balanced first, you can try the fancy tricks when you get more comfortable on the board.

2.   Know Which Foot Goes First

Once you're up on the board, figure out which foot you want to be forward. The two ways you can position your feet are "regular" and "goofy". The "regular" position is when the left foot is forward on the board and "goofy" is when the right foot leads. Don't let the names of the positions sway you to choose a certain way, both stances are totally normal, just choose to lead with whichever foot is more comfortable and feels natural.

3.   Control your Board

Once you are totally comfortable standing on the board, you can practice controlling the board. Controlling the board allows you to decide which way you are going and lays the foundation for future, more complicated, tricks. To control the board, you want to lean away from the boat, shift your weight to your heels, and "carve" through the water by transferring your weight to your toes and back again.

4.   Practice on Land

Thankfully, there are many ways to practice your wakeboard skills during the colder seasons that don't involve getting into freezing water. While on land, you can practice different balance exercises, like yoga, or you could invest in a balance board. A balance board is a board with a wheel in the middle that can be used indoors. To use it, you put your foot on either side of the board and try to stay stable to improve your balance. Once you get better at balance, you can also try doing tricks on

your balance board. This type of board improves your balance and strengthens your ankles, which will help you significantly once it's time to get back in the water. You can also practice on land through skateboarding or snowboarding. Both use similar muscles and can help you practice your balance, which lets you practice your skills on the off season.

5.   Lift More Weights

You might not think that lifting weights and getting stronger would help your wakeboarding skills, but it does. Wakeboarding uses so many muscles that you don't even think about- Biceps, abdominals, back, legs, forearms, etc. It truly is a sport that exercises the whole body, which is why it is important to strength train. Having strong muscles helps your balance on the board, your ability to do tricks, and allows you to get better faster than someone who does not weight train. Strength training also helps prevent injuries, as the stronger you are, the easier it will be to ride with correct form.

6.   Try some Tricks

Once you have the basics down, you can start practicing tricks. One of the most basic tricks is an Ollie. An ollie is simply a jump that you do while on the board. To do an ollie, get up on the board and begin riding. Once you feel comfortable on the board, shift your weight to your back leg and lift your front leg quickly, pushing off from the water from the back of the board. Once you're in the air, bring your back leg up to the same level as your front leg to level the board. When landing, try to keep the board flat, putting equal pressure on both of your feet. This keeps your board from braking and you from falling off. Once you perfect the ollie, you can start doing more complicated tricks.

Write a short story based on your summer experiences and get a chance to win $100 cash prize + 1 year free subscription to Lumos StepUp + trophy with a certificate.
To enter the competition follow the instructions.

Step 1

Visit **www.lumoslearning.com/a/tedbooks** and enter your access code to create
Lumos parent and student account.
Access Code : G7-8MLSLH-19562

Step 2

After registration, your child can upload their summer story by logging into the student portal and clicking on **Lumos Short Story Competition 2019.**

W8	Week 8
W9	Week 9
W10	Week 10
LSC	Lumos Short Story Competition 2019
	Lumos Short Story Competition 2019

Last date for submission is August 31, 2019

Use the space provided below for scratch work before uploading your summer story

Scratch Work

Summer Learning Activity Videos

Use the link below or QR code to watch the videos

http://lumoslearning.com/a/summervideos

   Beating the Summer Academic Loss

   Beating the Brain Drain through Literacy

   Beating the Brain Drain through Computing

   Warm-Up to a Great School Year

STOP! IN THE NAME OF EDUCATION: PREVENT SUMMER LEARNING LOSS WITH 7 SIMPLE STEPS

Summer Learning loss is defined as "a loss of knowledge and skills . . . most commonly due to . . . . extended breaks [during the summertime] " (from edglossary.org/learning-loss). Many teachers have certainly had the experience of taking the first month of school not only to introduce his or her rules and procedures to the class but also to get the kids back "up to speed" with thinking, remembering what they've learned . . . and in many cases, reviewing previous content. With a traditional school calendar, then, this can mean that up to 10% of the school year is spent playing catch-up.

What's a parent to do? Fortunately, there are some simple steps you can take with your child to help your son or daughter both enjoy the summer and keep those all-important skills honed and fresh:

(1) Read!

Research supports the relationship between independent reading and student achievement, so simply having your child read daily will make a positive difference. Check out the following sources to find books that your child will want to dive into: your public library, local bookstores, online stores (Amazon, Barnes and Noble, half.com, etc.), and yard sales (if the family hosting the sale has children a bit older than your own, you stand a good chance of scoring discarded books that are a perfect match for your son or daughter's reading level).

(2) Write!

Have your child write letters to out-of-town friends and family, or write postcards while on vacation. A summer journal is another way to document summer activities. For the artistic or tech-savvy child, you may choose to create a family scrapbook with captions (consider the online options at Shutterfly, Mixbook, and Smilebox). Not only will you preserve this summer's memories, but your child will also continue to practice his or her writing skills! (See Summer is Here! Ideas to Keep Your Child's Writing Skills Sharp for more writing ideas.)

(3) Do the Math!

Think of ways your child can incorporate math skills into daily activities: have a yard sale, and put

your child in charge of the cash box; help younger ones organize a lemonade stand (to practice salesmanship and making change). Or simply purchase a set of inexpensive flash cards to practice basic facts while waiting in line or on a long car ride. There's even a host of free online games that will keep your child's math skills sharp.

(4) "Homeschool" Your Child

Keeping your child's skills fresh doesn't have to cost a fortune: check out some of the Lumos Learning workbooks and online resources (at lumoslearning.com/store), and your child can work through several exercises each day. Even as little as twenty minutes a day can yield positive results, and it's easy to work in a small block of time here and there. For instance, your child can work in the book during a car ride, right before bedtime, etc. Or, simply make this part of your child's morning routine. For example: wake up, eat breakfast, complete chores, and then work in the workbook for 20 minutes. With time, you can make this a natural habit.

(5) Go Back-to-School Shopping (For a Great Summer School Learning Experience)

Check out offerings from the big names (think Sylvan, Huntington, Mathnasium, and Kumon), and also consider local summer schools. Some school districts and local colleges provide learning programs: research the offerings on-line for more information regarding the available options in your area.

(6) Take a Hike . . . Go Camping!

But "camp" doesn't always involve pitching a tent in the great outdoors. Nowadays, there are camps for every interest: sports camps, art camp, music camp, science camp, writing camp . . . the possibilities are endless! With a quick Internet search, you'll be able to turn up multiple options that will appeal to your son or daughter. And even if these camps aren't "academic", the life skills and interpersonal experiences are certain to help your child succeed in the "real world". For example, working together as a cast to put on a summer theater production involves memorizing lines, cooperation, stage crew coordination, and commitment – all skills that can come in handy when it comes to fostering a good work ethic and the ability to collaborate with others.

(7) Get tutored

Many teachers offer tutoring services throughout the summer months, either for individuals or small groups of students. Even the most school-averse student tends to enjoy the personal attention of a former teacher in a setting outside of the classroom. Plus, a tutor can tailor his or her instruction to pinpoint your child's needs – so you can maximize the tutoring sessions with the skills and concepts your child needs the most help with.

Of course, you don't need to do all seven steps to ensure that your child maintains his or her skills. Just following through with one or two of these options will go a long way toward continued learning, skills maintenance, and easing the transition to school when summer draws to a close.

SUMMER READING: QUESTIONS TO ASK THAT PROMOTE COMPREHENSION

As mentioned in our "Beating Summer Academic Loss" article, students are at risk of losing academic ground during the summer months, especially with respect to their reading level, spelling, and vocabulary. One of the best ways to prevent this "brain drain" for literacy is to have your son or daughter read each day during the summer break.

Better yet, you can promote these all-important skills and participate in your child's summer reading by engaging in active dialogue with your son or daughter. Below are several questions and ideas for discussion that will promote comprehension, recall, and critical thinking skills. In addition, these questions reflect several of the Common Core standards – which underpin the curriculum, instruction and standardized testing for most school districts. Of course, the standards vary by grade level, but some of the common themes that emerge in these standards are: citing evidence, summarizing, and making inferences.

• Citing evidence

Simply put, citing evidence involves going back into the text (book, magazine, newspaper, etc.) and finding "proof" to back up an answer, opinion, or assertion. For instance, you could ask your child, "Did you enjoy this book?" and then follow up that "yes" or "no" response with a "Why?" This requires the reader to provide details and examples from the story to support his or her opinion. For this particular question, then, your child may highlight plot events he or she liked, character attributes, writing style, and even genre (type of book) as evidence. Challenge for older students: Ask your child to go back into the text and find a direct quote to support an opinion or answer.

• Summarizing

For nonfiction pieces, this may involve being able to explain the 5W's – who, what, where, when, why (and how). For literature, ask your child to summarize the story elements, including: the setting, characters, main conflict or problem, events, resolution, and theme/lesson/moral. If your child can do this with specificity and accuracy, there's a very good chance that he or she comprehended the story. Challenge for older students: Ask your child to identify more complex story elements, such as the climax, rising action, and falling action.

• Making inferences

Making an inference is commonly referred to as "reading between the lines." That is, the reader can't find the answer to a question directly in the text but instead must synthesize or analyze information to come to a conclusion. To enhance these higher-level thinking skills, ask your child to describe the main character's personality, describe how a character changed by the end of a novel, or detail how the setting influenced the story's plot. Challenge for older students: Have the reader compare and contrast two or more characters to highlight similarities and differences in personality, actions, etc.

 Of course, if you read the same book that your child reads, you'll be able to come up with even more detailed questions – and also know if your child truly understood the reading based on his or her answers! But even if you don't get a chance to read what your child does, simply asking some of these questions not only helps your child's reading skills but also demonstrates an interest in your child – and his or her reading.

BEATING THE BRAIN DRAIN THROUGH COMPUTING: WEBINAR RECAP WITH PRINTABLE ACTIVITY SHEET

This past week, Lumos Learning hosted its second webinar in the "Beating the Brain Drain" series. During this interactive workshop, students were given many practical ideas and tips for keeping their math skills sharp in the summertime.

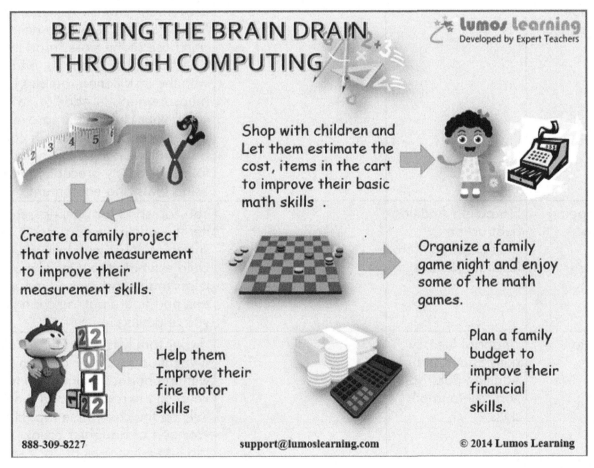

To review the webinar content, use this chart with your child to reinforce his or her math skills. Work together to select ideas that appeal to your son or daughter. And be sure to get involved: many of these suggestions are ideal for two or more people! Please note that there is an additional column so that you can keep track of and check off activities that your child has completed.

Suggested Activity	Skills/Mathematical Concepts	Completed this activity	Notes for parents
Create a family project that involves measurement, basic math calculations, geometry, etc.	Area Perimeter Measurement Basic facts		As a family, decide upon a project that you can do together. Possible project ideas include: creating a family garden, building a bird feeder, or tackling a home improvement project. Ask your child to help list the items you need to purchase at the store, read the directions (if applicable), and help with the installation, building, and measurement. In addition to math skills, your child can improve his or her fine motor skills. Of course, be sure to supervise properly and follow all safety precautions when using tools and equipment.
Go shopping together.	Estimation Addition Subtraction Multiplication Mental math skills		You can shop for back-to-school items – or simply go grocery shopping together. Have your child estimate the total cost of the items in the cart, determine sales tax, and figure out the change (if you're paying in cash).
Budget together.	Financial literacy skills Estimation Addition Subtraction Mental math skills		If your family is planning to take a vacation, ask your child to help with the budget! During the trip, keep all the receipts, and then tally up the cost of the trip. Have your son or daughter break up the trip into categories to track spending, too – food, fun, hotels, gas, etc. As a challenge, your child can calculate what percentage of the budget has been spent on each category.

Track family or individual spending.	Financial literacy skills Addition Subtraction Estimation		Use a blank checkbook register to monitor spending (real or imaginary). You child will need to learn how to document the date, event/item, withdrawals, deposits, and keep a running balance.
Host a family game night.	Skills will vary based on the game, but may include: Strategy Basic facts Making change Spatial awareness		Designate one evening each week as "family game night" and enjoy some of the following math games: Q-bitz, Bop It!, Monopoly, Qwirkle, Blokus, and Rummikub.
Download math apps and games.	Basic facts Algebra Geometry Mental math Flexible thinking Spatial awareness Reasoning Logic Strategy		Check out Google Play or the iTunes store for ideas. Some popular games include: 2048, Nozuku, TanZen, and Lumos Learning's StepUp App.

Ask your child to choose just three of the activities on the list to start with. Try to start the first activity as soon as possible – today, if time permits! – and then work the other activities into your daily routine as you see fit. By asking for your child's input, you'll have a better chance of him or her "buying into" the idea of reviewing math concepts during the summer months. With games, apps, and time with family built into these suggestions, though, you shouldn't have much difficulty convincing your child that math can actually be a lot of fun!

SUMMER IS HERE! KEEP YOUR CHILD'S WRITING SKILLS SHARP WITH ONLINE GAMES

Like Reading and math, free online activities exist for all subjects... and writing is no exception. Check out the following free interactive writing activities, puzzles, quizzes and games that reinforce writing skills and encourage creativity:

Primary Level (K-2nd Grade)

Story Writing Game

In this game, the child fills in the blanks of a short story. The challenge is for the storyteller to choose words that fit the kind of story that has been selected. For example, if the child chooses to tell a ghost story, then he or she must select words for each blank that would be appropriate for a scary tale. http://www.funenglishgames.com/writinggames/story.html

Opinions Quiz for Critical Thinking

Practice developing logical reasons to support a thesis with this interactive activity. Students read the stated opinion, such as, "We should have longer recess because..." The child must then select all of the possible reasons from a list that would support the given statement. The challenge lies

with the fact that each statement may have more than one possible answer, and to receive credit, the student must select all correct responses. This game is best suited for older primary students. http://www.netrover.com/~kingskid/Opinion/opinion.html

Interactives: Sequence

Allow your child to practice ordering events with this interactive version of the fairy tale, Cinderella. The child looks at several pictures from the story and must drag them to the bottom of the screen to put the events in chronological order. When the player mouses over each scene from the story, a sentence describing the image appears and is read aloud to the student. Once the events are in order, the student can learn more about plot and other story elements with the accompanying tutorials and lessons. http://www.learner.org/interactives/story/sequence.html

BEATING THE BRAIN DRAIN THROUGH LITERACY: WEBINAR RECAP WITH PRINTABLE ACTIVITY SHEET

This past week, Lumos Learning hosted a webinar for students: "Beating the Brain Drain Through Literacy." During this webinar, we provided the students with several ideas for keeping their literacy skills sharp in the summertime.

Here's a handy chart with the ideas from the webinar, ready for you to post on your refrigerator. Let your child pick and choose the activities that appeal to him or her. Of course, reading should be nonnegotiable, but the list below provides alternatives for reluctant readers – or for those who just don't enjoy reading a traditional fiction novel. The first set of activities touch upon ideas that reinforce writing skills, while the second half addresses reading skills. There is also room on the chart to date or check off activities your child has completed.

Skill Area	Activity	Completed this activity	Notes for parents
Writing skills, spelling, and/or vocabulary	Keep a journal (things you do, places you go, people you meet)		Even though journals work on spelling skills, be sure your child understands that spelling "doesn't count". Most children like to keep their journals private, so they don't need to worry about perfect skills or that someone else is going to read/grade what they wrote.
	Start a blog		Enable privacy settings to keep viewers limited to friends and family. Check out WordPress, Squarespace, and Quillpad to begin blogging.
	Get published		The following places publish student work: The Clairmont Review, CyberKids, Creative Kids Magazine, New Moon, and The Young Writer's Magazine.
	Write letters		Have your child write or type letters, postcards, and emails to friends and family members.
	Take part in a family movie night		Watch movies that are thought-provoking to elicit interesting post-movie discussions. Other good bets are movies that are based on a book (read the book first and compare the two).
	Organize a family game night		Choose word games to work on spelling and vocabulary skills (examples: Scrabble, Boggle, and Hangman).
Reading skills: fluency, comprehension, critical thinking, decoding skills,inferencing, etc.	Pick up a good book!		Places to find/buy/borrow books include: your public library, ebooks, yard sales, book stores, your child's school library (if it's open during the summer), and borrowed books from friends and family members.

	Read materials that aren't "books"…		Ideas include: karaoke lyrics, cereal boxes, newspapers, magazines for kids, billboards, close captioning, and audio books.
	Compete! Enter a reading challenge		Scholastic Reading hosts a competition called "Reading Under the Stars" to break a world record for minutes read. Barnes and Noble gives students the opportunity to earn one free book with "Imagination's Destination" reading challenge.

Note: Reading just six books over the summer can maintain – and sometimes even increase! – your child's reading level. Not sure if the book is appropriate for your child's reading level? Use the five-finger rule: have your son/daughter read a page of a book. Each time your child encounters a word that is unfamiliar or unknown, he or she holds up a finger. If your child holds up more than five fingers on a given page, that book is probably too difficult.

However, there are some books that a child will successfully tackle if it's high-interest to him or her. Keep in mind that reading levels are a guide (as is the five-finger rule), and some children may exceed expectations…so don't hold your child back if he or she really wants to read a particular book (even if it may appear to be too challenging).

Remember, if students do some of these simple activities, they can prevent the typical four to six weeks of learning loss due to the "summer slide." And since spelling, vocabulary and reading skills are vulnerable areas, be sure to encourage your child to maintain his or her current literacy level…it will go a long way come September!

WEBINAR "CLIFF NOTES" FOR BEATING SUMMER ACADEMIC LOSS: AN INFORMATIVE GUIDE TO PARENTS

The "Summer Slide"

First, it's important to understand the implications of "summer slide" – otherwise known as summer learning loss. Research has shown that some students who take standardized tests in the fall could have lost up to 4-6 weeks of learning each school year (when compared with test results from the previous spring). This means that teachers end up dedicating the first month of each new school year for reviewing material before they can move onto any new content and concepts.

The three areas that suffer most from summer learning loss are in the areas of vocabulary/reading, spelling, and math. In Stop! In the Name of Education: Prevent Summer Learning Loss With 7 Simple Steps, we discussed some activities parents could use with children to prevent summer slide. Let's add to that list with even more ways to keep children engaged and learning – all summer long.

Be sure to check out:

•Your Child's School

Talk to child's teacher, and tell him or her that you'd like to work on your child's academics over the summer. Most teachers will have many suggestions for you.

In addition to the classroom teacher as a resource, talk to the front office staff and guidance counselors. Reading lists and summer programs that are organized through the school district may be available for your family, and these staff members can usually point you in the right direction.

•Your Community

A quick Google search for "free activities for kids in (insert your town's name)" will yield results of possible educational experiences and opportunities in your area. Some towns offer "dollar days", park lunches, and local arts and entertainment.

You may even wish to involve your child in the research process to find fun, affordable memberships and discounts to use at area attractions. For New Jerseyans and Coloradans, check out www.funnewjersey.com and www.colorado.com for ideas.

Of course, don't forget your local library! In addition to books, you can borrow movies and audiobooks, check out the latest issue of your favorite magazine, and get free Internet access on the library's computers. Most libraries offer a plethora of other educational choices, too – from book clubs and author visits to movie nights and crafts classes, you're sure to find something at your local branch that your child will enjoy.

•Stores

This is an extremely engaging activity – and your child won't even know he or she is learning! For grocery shopping, ask your child to write the list while you dictate. At the store, your son/daughter can locate the items and keep a cost tally to stay within a specified budget. At the checkout, you can have a contest to see whose estimate of the final bill is most accurate – and then reward the winner!

You may wish to plan a home improvement project or plant a garden: for this, your child can make the list, research the necessary materials, and then plan and execute the project after a visit to your local home improvement store. All of these activities involve those three critical areas of spelling, vocabulary/reading, and math.

•The Kitchen

This is one of the best places to try new things – by researching new foods, recipes, and discussing healthy food choices – while practicing math skills (such as measuring ingredients, doubling recipes, etc.). Your child may also enjoy reading about new cultures and ethnicities and then trying out some new menu items from those cultures.

•The Television

TV doesn't have to be mind numbing … when used appropriately. You can watch sports with your child to review stats and make predictions; watch documentaries; or tune into the History Channel, Discovery, National Geographic, HGTV, and more. Anything that teaches, helps your child discover new interests, and promotes learning new things together is fair game.

As an extension, you may decide to research whether or not the show portrays accurate information. And for those children who really get "into" a certain topic, you can enrich their learning by taking related trips to the museum, doing Internet research, and checking out books from the library that tie into the topic of interest.

•Movies

Movies can be educational, too, if you debrief with your child afterwards. Schedule a family movie

night, and then discuss how realistic the movie was, what the messages were, etc.

For book-based movies (such as Judy Moody, Harry Potter, Percy Jackson, etc.), you could read the book together first, and then view the movie version. Comparing and contrasting the two is another terrific educational way to enjoy time together and work on your child's reasoning skills.

Note: www.imdb.com and www.commonsensemedia.org are great sites for movie recommendations and movie reviews for kids and families.

•Games

Playing games promotes taking turns, reading and math skills, and strategy development. Scour yard sales for affordable board games like Scrabble, Monopoly, Uno, Battleship, and Qwirkle.

Don't forget about non-board games, like those found on the Wii, Nintendo, Xbox, and other gaming consoles. You'll still want to choose wisely and limit your child's screen time, but these electronic versions of popular (and new) games mirror the way kids think ... while focusing on reading and math skills. For more ideas, Google "education apps" for suggestions.

•Books, books, books!

Of course, nothing beats reading for maintaining skills. When you can connect your child with a book that is of interest to him or her, it can be fun for your child, build confidence, and improve fluency.

To help your child find a book that's "just right", use the five-finger rule: choose a page from a possible book and have your child read that page. Every time he or she encounters an unknown word, put up a finger. If your child exceeds five fingers (that is, five unknown words), that book is probably too challenging and he or she may wish to pass on it.

For reluctant readers, consider non-book reading options, like:magazines (such as Ranger Rick, American Girl, Discovery Kids, and Sports Illustrated for Kids), cereal boxes, billboards, current events, closed captioning, and karaoke. If you keep your eyes open, you'll find there are many natural reading opportunities that surround us every day.

Whatever you do, remember to keep it fun. Summer is a time for rest and rejuvenation, and learning doesn't always have to be scheduled. In fact, some of the most educational experiences are unplanned.

Visit lumoslearning.com/parents/summer-program for more information.

Valuable Learning Experiences: A Summer Activity Guide for Parents

Soon school will be out of session, leaving the summer free for adventure and relaxation. However, it's important to also use the summer for learning activities. Giving your son or daughter opportunities to keep learning can result in more maturity, self-growth, curiosity, and intelligence. Read on to learn some ways to make the most of this summer.

Read

Summer is the perfect time to get some extra reading accomplished. Youth can explore books about history, art, animals, and other interests, or they can read classic novels that have influenced people for decades. A lot of libraries have summer fun reading programs which give children, teens, and adults little weekly prizes for reading books. You can also offer a reward, like a $25 gift card, if your child reads a certain amount of books.

Travel

"The World is a book and those who do not travel read only a page." This quote by Saint Augustine illustrates why travel is so important for a student (and even you!). Travel opens our eyes to new cultures, experiences, and challenges. When you travel, you see commonalities and differences between cultures.

Professor Adam Galinsky of Columbia Business School, who has researched travel benefits, said in a Quartz article that travel can help a child develop compassion and empathy: "Engaging with another culture helps kids recognize that their own egocentric way of looking at the world is not the only way of being in the world."

If the student in your life constantly complains about not having the newest iPhone, how would they feel seeing a child in a third-world country with few possessions? If you child is disrespectful and self-centered, what would they learn going to Japan and seeing a culture that promotes respect and otherness instead of self-centeredness?

If you can't afford to travel to another country, start a family travel fund everyone can contribute to and in the meantime, travel somewhere new locally! Many people stay in the area they live instead of exploring. Research attractions in your state and nearby states to plan a short road trip to fun and educational places!

Visit Museums

You can always take your children to visit museums. Spending some quality time at a museum can enhance curiosity because children can learn new things, explore their interests, or see exhibits expanding upon school subjects they recently studied. Many museums have seasonal exhibits, so research special exhibits nearby. For example, "Titanic: The Artifact Exhibition" has been making its way to various museums in the United States. It contains items recovered from the Titanic as well as interactive activities and displays explaining the doomed ship's history and tragic demise. This year, the exhibit is visiting Las Vegas, Orlando, and Waco.

Work

A final learning suggestion for the summer is for students to get a job, internship, or volunteer position. Such jobs can help with exploring career options. For example, if your child is thinking of becoming a vet, they could walk dogs for neighbors, or if your child wants to start their own business, summer is the perfect time to make and sell products.

Not only will a job or volunteer work look good on college applications, but it will also teach your children valuable life lessons that can result in more maturity and responsibility. You could enhance the experience by teaching them accounting and illustrating real world problems to them, like budgeting money for savings and bills.

The above suggestions are just four of the many ways you can help learning continue for your child or children all summer long. Experience and seeing things first-hand are some of the most important ways that students can learn, so we hope you find the above suggestions helpful in designing a fun, educational, and rewarding summer that will have benefits in and out of the classroom.

Additional Information

What if I buy more than one Lumos Study Program?

Step 1
Visit the URL and login to your account.
http://www.lumoslearning.com

Step 2
Click on 'My tedBooks' under the "Account" tab.
Place the Book Access Code and submit.

Step 3
To add the new book for a registered student, choose the
○ Existing Student button and select the student and submit.

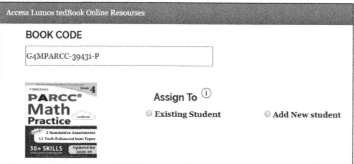

To add the new book for a new student, choose the ○ Add New student
button and complete the student registration.

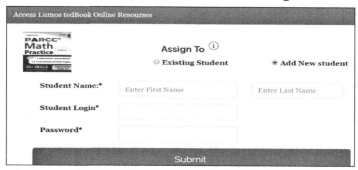

Lumos StepUp® Mobile App FAQ For Students

What is the Lumos StepUp® App?

It is a FREE application you can download onto your Android Smartphones, tablets, iPhones, and iPads.

What are the Benefits of the StepUp® App?

This mobile application gives convenient access to Practice Tests, Common Core State Standards, Online Workbooks, and learning resources through your Smartphone and tablet computers.

- Eleven Technology enhanced question types in both MATH and ELA
- Sample questions for Arithmetic drills
- Standard specific sample questions
- Instant access to the Common Core State Standards
- Jokes and cartoons to make learning fun!

Do I Need the StepUp® App to Access Online Workbooks?

No, you can access Lumos StepUp® Online Workbooks through a personal computer. The StepUp® app simply enhances your learning experience and allows you to conveniently access StepUp® Online Workbooks and additional resources through your smart phone or tablet.

How can I Download the App?

Visit **lumoslearning.com/a/stepup-app** using your Smartphone or tablet and follow the instructions to download the app.

**QR Code
for Smartphone
Or Tablet Users**

Lumos StepUp® Mobile App FAQ For Parents and Teachers

What is the Lumos StepUp® App?

It is a free app that teachers can use to easily access real-time student activity information as well as assign learning resources to students. Parents can also use it to easily access school-related information such as homework assigned by teachers and PTA meetings. It can be downloaded onto smart phones and tablets from popular App Stores.

What are the Benefits of the Lumos StepUp® App?

It provides convenient access to

- Standards aligned learning resources for your students
- An easy to use Dashboard
- Student progress reports
- Active and inactive students in your classroom
- Professional development information
- Educational Blogs

How can I Download the App?

Visit **lumoslearning.com/a/stepup-app** using your Smartphone or tablet and follow the instructions to download the app.

**QR Code
for Smartphone
Or Tablet Users**

Other Books By Lumos Learning For Grade 8

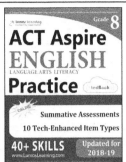

ACT Aspire Math & ELA Practice Book

CMAS Math & ELA Practice Book

FSA Math & ELA Practice Book

GMAS Math & ELA Practice Book

ILEARN Math & ELA Practice Book

LEAP Math & ELA Practice Book

MS MAAP Math & ELA Practice Book

MO MAAP Math & ELA Practice Book

Other Books By Lumos Learning For Grade 8

MCAS Math & ELA Practice Book

NYST Math & ELA Practice Book

OST Math & ELA Practice Book

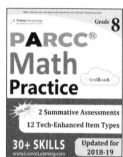

PARCC Math & ELA Practice Book

SBAC Math & ELA Practice Book

Available
- At Leading book stores
- www.lumoslearning.com/a/lumostedbooks